1979

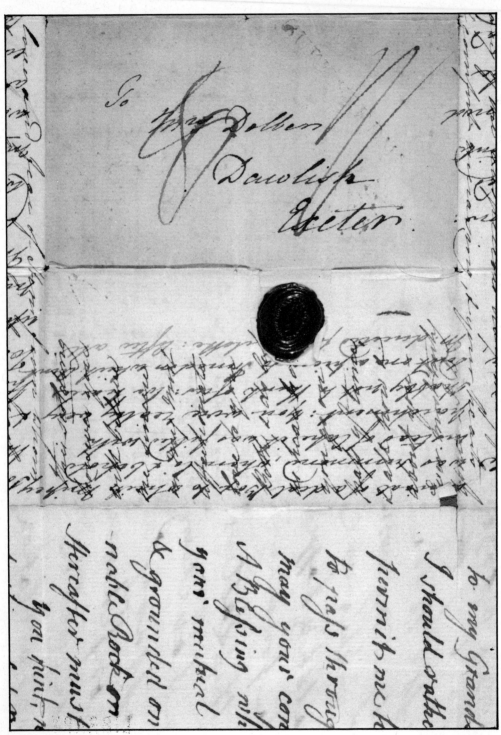

To
Mrs Dolben
Dawlish
Exeter

INTERPRETING HANDWRITING

JANE PATERSON

David McKay Company, Inc.
New York

Acknowledgements
The publishers are grateful to the following for their permission to reproduce illustrations:
BBC: p. 17; J. E. Ciriot *Dictionary of Symbols:* p. 35;
Edward Clodd *History of the Alphabet* (George Newnes): pp. 12–13;
Cook *Tree of Life:* p. 38; David Diringer *Writing* (Thames and Hudson): p. 10; C. M. Dixon: pp. 46–47;
British Gas: p. 15br, p. 15bl; Derek Hudson *Munby: Man of Two Worlds* (John Murray): p. 65;
John R. Freeman and the Master and Fellows of Trinity College, Cambridge: p. 65;
Keystone Press: p. 67; C. J. W. Olliver *An Analysis of Magic and Witchcraft* (Rider and Co): p.35;
Photoresources: pp. 42–3; Popperfoto: p. 36; Times Newspapers: p. 16;
US National Aeronautics and Space Administration: p. 15t;
Roger Wood: p. 55.

The Postscript to 'Prologue: The Birth of Architecture' on p. 50 is
reprinted by permission of Faber and Faber Ltd and of Random House Inc
from *About the House* by W. H. Auden.

The author would like to thank Beryl Kearsey, Jo Nicholl, John Price, and
Marty and Will Stewart for their very kind help with this book, and all
the members of Mensa who so kindly completed the anonymous survey from
which a number of examples of writing are taken. In the case of some
of the signatures that appear in this book the author has been unable to
trace the writers to ask for their permission. She would like to crave
their indulgence for the liberty she has taken and take this opportunity
of thanking them. When comparing their own handwriting with the samples
in this book readers should be aware that sometimes handwriting samples have been reduced.
Those that have been reduced are marked with an asterisk.

Title page: A letter of 1812

First American Edition, 1976

Library of Congress Catalog Card Number: 76-28576
ISBN 0-679-50700-0 (cloth)
ISBN 0-679-50701-9 (paper)

Printed in Great Britain

Contents

Introduction

Handwriting is frozen gesture—an expression of the personality of the writer and of what he is trying to communicate. The study of the special relationship between handwriting and personality is called graphology. (It is not the study of maps and graphs, nor is it in any way connected with calligraphy, which is the artistic discipline of penmanship and beautiful styles of writing.)

Beginning with a look at man's early endeavours with symbols and picture writing, this book goes on to show the reader how to study handwriting, and how to assess the psychological implications of different kinds of writing. Personality is so varied and diverse that this is a field of detection and exploration without limit.

All our lives the most trouble we have is with ourselves and yet we are somehow too 'near' to see ourselves in focus. Very few of us have any degree of self-knowledge, self-awareness or insight into our own personalities. It is much easier to criticize others than to be self-critical. Analysing handwriting helps us to understand ourselves as well as others.

1 Signs and Symbols

We are living in what might be called the Plectromatic Age, this word being an amalgam of Plastic, Electronic and Automatic. It could also be called the Plectraumatic Age, because it is a time in history of drastic upheaval and change.

The spotlight of television communication covers all corners of the globe. If students are rioting in Tokyo, we are visually concerned with the situation the same day in London. We are involved in all happenings, sporting and tragic, however local. If there is a train crash, we are all there, intimately at the scene, involved and talking to the victims. The personal suffering of individuals is invaded by the camera, sometimes in a heartless way. Their personal emotion and grief belong to and are shared by us all, and whether it is an eviction, a funeral, a wedding, we are there.

Ever since the invention of the wheel, man has been developing or extending his faculties. First he walked on foot, then came the wheel, which meant he moved faster and further, in the bullock-cart or the carriage. This led to the train, the car, the aeroplane, and now Concorde. He also extended the ear with the wireless, the telephone, morse code and radio telephone, so he could hear faster and further; he extended the eye with telescopes, binoculars, and now, television. Each of these extensions has increased the speed and distance of man's ability to communicate. The world has become smaller and smaller.

Now we have the computer which is an extension of the brain and has again vastly accelerated the whole process. Electric technology is circuiting every aspect of our lives. The world, as Marshall McLuhan tells us, has become a global village; we are irrevocably involved with each other.

In recent times there has awakened an awareness in modern man that he is a part of nature, and that he ignores this at his peril. Primitive man lived with nature; he had to know the habits, environments and subtle movements of all living things in order to survive. He had a wisdom, being a part of nature himself, that we have lost. Now at the present time there is a movement among young people to go back and search for past wisdom.

In this book we are concerned with handwriting. Writing is a means of communication. For social animals an efficient means of communication is essential and this is achieved by facial grimaces, body and tail movements, grunts, shouts and smells. Man's potential as a social group was greatly extended once he had achieved the ability to talk; before this he could presumably only communicate visually by facial gestures and expressions, frowns, scowls, leers, nods, shrugs, warding off and beckoning, come hither gestures, waving, crying, smiling, laughing, cringing, pleading and submissive gestures, acknowledging defeat, disdain, showing fear, surprise, delight, welcome and dancing with joy.

He could communicate orally by whistling, humming, singing, tapping, beating drums and clapping; and tactually, by clasping and shaking hands, back and chest slapping, stroking and grooming. Personal contact by touch has declined in modern man; children are continually told 'not to touch' so the desire for tactile experience is there but it is inhibited by society.

People in Britain today appear to spend more time stroking their dogs and cats than their husbands, wives and families. Babies get touched, but they do not get the continual body contact from European 'educated' mothers that they would get from primitive 'earth' mothers. Certainly shaking hands and back slapping are still with us and so is 'grooming' in the guise of hairdressing, massage and beauty salons. The personal attention given and physical contact of hairdressing can be therapeutic to lonely isolated people who have no-one at home with whom to communicate and who are really 'out of touch'.

Primitive man very likely also communicated by smell. Social animals have numerous systems for marking territories and boundaries by scent, by either urinating or rubbing themselves against branches. Smell is a sense that modern man has not extended, but which is universally used in the animal kingdom. In fact, man does his best to eliminate it, with the many deodorants that are on the market. What kind of new world might be discovered with the invention of a strong smell magnifier! Primitive people can be interested in whether a stranger 'smells good'. If a new bride arrives in the family this can be a talking point, and certainly many diseases give a clear indication of their presence by the curious smell emanating from the sufferer.

Figure 1

Once man could talk he could express emotions more clearly. The conception of time, past, present and future, was refined with language. Also with speech came the importance of remembering what was said. One of the first memory recording devices was a belt which had knotted strings or thongs running down each side. Fig. 1 is a picture of one used in Peru; it is called a quipus.

The strings or cords and their knots on the quipus could be in different colours. One can conceive that an 'accountant' of the time might have had a string for each client, a knot of one colour standing for single units, another for tens, etc; perhaps another string or colour meant debts. Possibly he had his dubious clients on the left of his quipus and the important ones on the right. In the same way the 'town clerk' could record important civic events, special days, festivals and calendar months on his quipus. A personal quipus could remind the owner how old he was or particulars about his family, personal possessions and domestic animals.

Herodotus tells us how Darius, much later, used knots to give instructions to some men of Ionia who were to guard a bridge which spanned the Ister for sixty days, while he marched on towards Scythis. After showing them a leather thong with sixty knots tied in it, he said, 'Untie one knot each day. If I do not return before the last knot is untied you may then sail away to your own

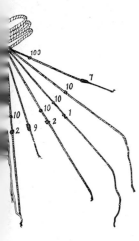

lands.' The present day legacies of this system are the rosary and the knot we hopefully tie in our handkerchief to remind us not to forget some important event.

Centuries later, but still in a primitive world, American Indians developed a code of sign communications well known to boy scouts and trackers. Fenimore Cooper's stories of the Indians recall how ingenious they were at communicating by giving and receiving silent signals. If they were following a trail and wanted to inform Indians coming later of their movements, marks were left along the trail. These were made with whatever the terrain provided, either stones, leaves, grass or marks cut in the bark of tree trunks.

If the track lay straight ahead it would be marked thus:

If an indication of a turn to the right was required:

If a turn to the left:

Sometimes they fixed up a more permanent sign board with branches and twigs, which were adjusted according to events:

 I am going East

 I have not gone far

 I have gone far

 I have gone off on a five days' journey

Two sticks crossed meant, 'Do not go further on this path.' A circle drawn on the ground with a stone in it meant, 'I have gone home.'

They also communicated by smoke signals:

Ŷ The camp is here   ᎤᎤ I am lost

ᎤᎤᎤ Good news   ᎤᎤᎤᎤ Summons to meet

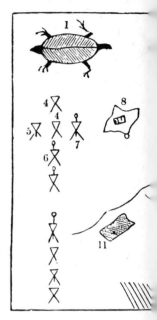

Figure 3

The signs of Indians led to a wider aspect of visual signalling, 'informing' by pictures. A similar situation to the one mentioned above, where a couple of crossed sticks were used, was found in New Mexico. An Indian rock drawing was found near a very precipitous trail; the drawing consisted of a mountain goat standing upright and a man riding a horse upside-down. The message to be conveyed was that although the track was suitable for a mountain goat, a rider would very likely come to grief and end up as the picture showed.

All over the world man has left a legacy of his aesthetic sense, in cave and rock drawings, pictures of himself and the animals that inhabited his world. These pictures were drawn to tell a story of the hunt or of a special leader, or else they conveyed a message or recorded the seasons.

The pictures that told a story were called pictographs. Edward Clodd's book, *The History of the Alphabet,* shows an excellent example from the American Indians (Fig. 2). This picture is a copy of a petition sent by a group of Indian Tribes to the United States Congress for fishing rights in some small lakes near Lake Superior. The leading tribe is represented by Oshcabawis, on the extreme right of the picture, whose totem is the 'Crane'. Behind him are Waimitligzhig and Ogemagee and a third Indian, all of the 'Marten' totem. Then follows Little Elk of the 'Bear' totem, and then a delegate from the 'Manfish' totem and finally an Indian representing the 'Catfish' totem. Lines connect each eye and each heart of every totem to the eye and heart of the leader of the 'Crane' totem. This indicates that they, and all the Indians that they represent, are all of the same heart or feel the same, and they are all of the same

Figure 2

12

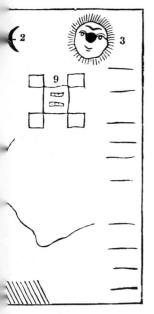

mind or see the same. A further line or thread of thought connects the 'Crane' with the lakes where the tribes want to fish, and yet another line runs forward from the 'Crane' to the place where their thoughts are directed and the people to whom their petition is presented: the United States Congress.

The picture shown in Fig. 3 gives the biography of Wingemund, a well-known Delaware Chief. The numbers on the picture indicate (1) the 'Tortoise' totem of the tribe, (2) the individual totem or sign of the Chief, (3) the sun which shone on the strokes beneath, which represent the ten expeditions in which Wingemund took part; on the left of the picture (4), (5), (6), (7) are the prisoners taken, clearly indicated as either male or female, and also the number killed—these are drawn headless. In the centre of the picture (8), (9), (10), (11) are sketches of the position attacked and the slanting strokes at the bottom refer to the number of Wingemund's followers.

The picture in Fig. 4 is a copy, reduced in size, of a love-letter drawn on birch bark which an Ojibwa girl sent to her sweet-heart at White Earth, Minnesota. She was of the 'Bear' totem and he of the 'Mud Puppy' totem. These are identified on the left of the picture and represent the girl and her lover. The two lines indicating paths from their tribal camps meet and continue on one track to a point between two lakes. Another trail branches off on the left towards two tents. The three crosses indicate that the three girls encamped here are Catholic converts. The left tent has an opening from which a hand is visible making a beckoning gesture. The arm represents the writer who is making the Indian sign of welcome to her lover. This is done by holding the palm of the hand down and forward and drawing the extended index finger towards the place occupied by the speaker, showing the path upon the ground to be followed by the person called.'

Figure 4

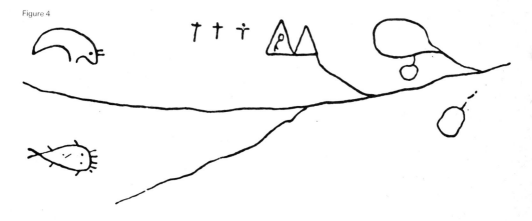

The pictographs and the American Indian signs were visual images in no way connected with speech or language. The next step forward in development of visual/verbal communication was the marriage of sound or language with written signs. This was called phonetization, which started by way of the 'rebus'. The dictionary defines 'rebus' as 'enigmatic representation of a name or word by pictures suggesting its syllables.'

A rebus is also a pun, playing on the double meaning of words. The word 'saw' can mean a saw with which to saw wood, or the past tense of the verb 'to see'. The word 'box' can mean a container or the verb 'to box'. 'Saw' can be illustrated by a picture of a saw. The word 'bee' or 'be' can be indicated by a picture of a bee whether it means the insect or the verb 'to be'. A picture of an eye can mean either an eye or the word 'I'.

In this way we can construct an easily-read sentence:

'Eye bee leaf eye saw baby swallow safety pin.'

Egyptian hieroglyphic writing was developed on this basis. In the *Scientific American* (September 1972) E. H. Gombrich showed the name of the god Osiris written in hieroglyphics as a rebus, with a throne and an eye, to which is adjoined a picture of a divine sceptre. Another version of the rebus is shown in Figure 5 on pp. 42–3.

Symbols can convey relationships more quickly and more subtly than a string of words and are still used at the present time. The bee is a symbol of 'industry' and J. E. Roberts draws attention to the fact that the bee appears in the coat-of-arms of nine industrial towns in Lancashire, of Luton in Bedfordshire and Aylesbury in Buckinghamshire. The coat-of-arms of Barrow-in-Furness consists of gules (red) on a gold band (diagonal bar across), and an arrow pointing upwards towards a bee. It is an heraldic pun, or rebus: add 'bee' to 'arrow' and the name is there. There is a ship above this to denote the type of industry and the 'arms' of the local gentry who helped to make the town prosperous.

Symbols are again becoming more universal; road signs and their meaning are easily comprehended, as are the signs (Fig. 6) used at the Olympic Games in Mexico 1968, where many nationalities, speaking numerous different languages, were gathered.

The symbolic picture adopted for North Sea Gas in Britain is also interesting (Figs. 7 and 8). Neptune is the outer planet of our solar system; its symbol is the trident. Neptune is also the god of the sea, and his symbol is also the trident. The trident has been called the magic wand used in water divining, so it is very significant to use the trident coming out of the sea, burning with the vitality of North Sea Gas, thus symbolically combining past myths with the present.

Figure 6

Figures 7 and 8

NATURAL GAS

CONVERSION

In early cuneiform writing, written on clay, these symbols were used:

to go

heaven

fish

In Egyptian hieroglyphics:

welcome, the cup of hospitality

I am at home

the sinking sun, death

In Chinese symbols:

a child

a man

a woman

rain

The Times 'European Shopping Basket', which compares prices of various food commodities throughout Europe, has these symbols at the head of columns with comparative prices:

rumpsteak | pork chops | potatoes | butter | margarine | cheese | chicken | fresh cod | bread | milk

The symbol shown on the left has recently appeared; it represents a person reading an open book, and has been devised by the Adult Literacy Resource Agency, the BBC and the National Committee for Adult Literacy, to help Britain's two million adults who cannot read and write to recognize where they can find help. Perhaps an electronic symbol language will some day be developed that can be understood quite easily by all nationalities as well as by people who have difficulty mastering alphabetical language.

Now let us get back to the development of writing, which we had left at the stage where signs expressed words and syllables. There were four main writings of this type, Sumerian, Egyptian, Hittite and Chinese. From the Egyptian hieroglyphics developed the West Semitic, syllabic writings of which Hebrew and Aramaic are examples. These in turn developed into the alphabetic writings—writing that expresses single sounds—such as Greek and Latin. Hundreds of alphabets throughout the world, although they appear diverse, use the principles first established in Greek writing.

David Diringer says 'writing is the graphic counterpart of speech, the "fixing" of spoken language in a permanent form. By means of it, language is made capable of transcending the ordinary condition of time and space. Writing was held in such esteem, it was attributed as a gift of the gods'.

Legend certainly holds 'Thoth' (Fig. 9, p. 55), the Ibis-headed god of the Nile, to be the Egyptian inventor of writing. It is said that he scraped with his bill upon the muddy banks of the river and the first sacred characters evolved. Primitive people were in awe of the written word; the ability to write brought power. The Smithsonian Report, 1864, tells a story of an Indian who was sent by a missionary to a colleague with four loaves of bread, accompanied by a letter stating their number. The Indian ate one of the loaves and was, of course, found out. He was sent on a similar errand and repeated the theft but took the precaution to hide the letter under a stone while he was eating the bread so that it might not see him!

Without the ability to write, mankind would have no history, other than orally-transmitted tales and myths, and no technology. Dolphins have a superior intelligence and have evolved a complicated language to communicate, but it is the ability to write which has set man apart.

The pen

The word pen comes from the Latin word *penna,* a feather. One of the first writing implements was a stylus which was used to engrave on clay tablets or tablets smeared with wax. We still talk of a 'style of writing'. Another early writing tool was the reed. This could be filled with different liquids; one mixture used was soot combined with lamp-oil and musk to neutralize the unsavoury smell.

Quill pens were introduced about the sixth century BC. Goose quills were the most popular but swan and turkey quills were also used. At one time, according to the *Encyclopaedia Britannica,* imports into Great Britain were 30,000,000 quills annually, the best coming from Holland and Russia.

Steel point pens were tried out in Birmingham in about 1780, but there is evidence that metal pens have an earlier history; according to Edward Clodd one with a split nib was found by Dr Waldstein in a tomb of the third century BC at Eretria, on the island of Euboea in the Aegean.

The early nineteenth century saw the arrival of fountain pens but they did not become really popular until the Waterman pens of New York in 1884. The first patent for a ball-type dispenser was issued in October 1888 to John Loud, an American. During World War II improved methods for grinding and measuring balls for ball bearings were devised and these were adapted for the manufacture of ball-point pens. Lazlo Biro, a Hungarian living in Argentina, was the first to make a satisfactory ball-point pen in about 1944.

Paper

The word paper comes from 'papyrus', a water plant of the sedge family that was cultivated and once grew in abundance in the delta of the river Nile. The *Encyclopaedia Britannica* gives a description of the rush 'papyrus' which is now extinct in lower Egypt. We learn that it grew about three feet high and that its main root was the thickness of a man's wrist. The head of the plant was made into garlands for the shrines of the gods and the wood of the root was used for fuel as well as for making various utensils. The pith of the plant was eaten both cooked and in its natural state. The stem was used for boat building and sails, and also for mats, cloth, cords and writing material. The writing material was made from the stem of the plant, cut into long strips. These strips were laid on a board, side by side, and another layer of shorter strips was laid at right angles. The sheet so formed was soaked in the Nile water and then hammered and dried in the sun. Any roughness was polished with ivory or a smooth shell. To form a roll of papyrus, several sheets were joined together. Medieval Latin manuscripts on papyrus still exist in libraries in Europe.

From the very early times that we have been thinking about, there was nothing instinctive about handwriting. It was a craft that had to be learnt, an expertise requiring personal control, perseverance and manual dexterity. In any form of manual skill or artistic creation achieved by man, something entirely unique emanating from the individual goes into the work. Art experts are able to identify the 'style' of a master. In fashion, leading designers create their own 'style'. Tennis players, all endeavouring to produce the same results of expertise at the game, each take on to the court their own way of playing; some awkward, lacking grace, but with an accurate, penetrating force and ambitious determination; others with movements that flow with harmony and rhythm, a sheer physical perfection and integration of body movements that is a joy to watch; others move with abandon but lack control and co-ordination so results are erratic; still others tie themselves into knots and contortions when producing a serve. Personality leaves its hallmark on whatever we do and so it is with handwriting.

Handwriting and personality

The study of human personality from handwriting is called graphology. An interest in the connection between handwriting and personality recurs throughout history. Aristotle and the Roman historian Suetonius Tranquillus are quoted as having shown interest in the subject, the latter in his work *Lives of the Caesars.* John Keats is quoted as saying in a letter, 'I am convinced more and more day by day that fine writing is next to fine doing, the top thing in the world.' Disraeli, Goethe, Robert Browning and Baudelaire all flirted with the subject, which was intermittently a fashionable intellectual pursuit in Europe at the time. Sir Walter Scott obviously had serious thoughts on the matter. The following is a quotation from his book *Chronicles of Canongate:* 'Nay, my first impression was to thrust it into the fire . . . a little reflection made me ashamed of this feeling of impatience, and as I looked at the even, concise, yet tremulous hand in which the manuscript was written, I could not help thinking, according to an opinion I have heard seriously maintained, that something of a man's character may be conjectured from his handwriting. That neat, but crowded and constrained, small hand argued a man of a good conscience, well-regulated passions, and, to use his own phrase, an upright walk in life, but it also indicated narrowness of spirit, inveterate prejudice, and hinted at some degree of intolerance, which though not natural to the disposition, had arisen out of a limited education. The passages from Scripture and the classics, rather profanely than happily introduced, and written in a half-text character to mark their importance, illustrated that peculiar sort of pedantry which always considers the argument as gained if secured by a quotation.'

Around 1840, a pioneer movement of interest in the subject developed in France through the studies of the Abbé Flandrin and the Abbé Jean-Hippolyte Michon; the latter spent many years of his life making a dossier of handwriting and the personality quirks of the writers. He coined the word 'graphology' and after the publication of his books *Les Mystères de l'Écriture* and *La Methode Pratique de Graphologie* there was a great deal of interest in the subject in France.

With the end of the nineteenth century, the focal point of interest in graphology moved from France to Germany. Dr Ludwig Klages, who had already published several works on philosophy, wrote five books on graphology and became the leading force in Germany on the matter. Now in the second half of the twentieth century (to quote from *Handwriting Analysis in Business*), 'Handwriting analysis is, and has been for many years, accepted in Germany as a valid subject for scientific study and as a commonplace tool for use in the business of personnel selection and vocational guidance. Its accepted status in the academic sphere is easy to substantiate. In many universities—among them Berlin, Bonn, Cologne, Freiburg, Heidelberg, Kiel, Mainz and Munich—graphology either forms part of the medical faculty, or has been incorporated in psychology courses. In Hamburg the study is part of the medical faculty, for the simple reason that the late Professor Rudolf Pophal, a pioneer graphologist of international fame, was originally a medical man. As a rule, students reading psychology may take an examination in graphology as an addition to their diploma as qualified practising psychologists. In consequence, knowledge and practice of the subject is widespread among psychotherapists, sociologists and teachers, as well as among educational research workers dealing with problem individuals and groups. The Graphological Diploma Courses take three years to complete, and the diploma is awarded as the result of passing exhaustive written and verbal tests.'

In Britain the subject has made little perceptible advance in the last fifteen years. Most mature Englishmen are sceptical and wary of the subject, but young people, unfettered by prejudice, can see the potential.

Graphology is a science and an art, as is all applied psychology and medicine. Pure graphology is a science; writing is fixed and measurable, research into writing sizes, proportions and angles with reference to age, sex, and profession is a science and produces facts. However, most graphologists work with reports which are composed of words. It is extremely difficult to transpose findings, however scientific, into comprehensible, clear, concise language that anyone can understand; it is a gift given to few people, and this is where misunderstandings can lead the subject into disrepute.

There is also a strong instinctive inhibiting mechanism in man with regard to research into personality and perhaps, as in all new aspects of learning, change produces insecurity. Professor Laithwaite, on a television programme, spoke of the 'abominable no men'. These were people who knew his experiments were useless without finding out what they were about or reading any material on the subject. Graphology is dogged by 'abominable no men' of this exact variety, their feelings mostly induced by an undercurrent of personal insecurity and fear.

This book hopes to allay that fear and illustrate how graphology works and what a wonderful potential for help and personal exploration it can be. It is an immensely complex subject and one in which learning never ceases because of the uniqueness of each individual's writing. Writing is, in effect, frozen gesture; all individual gesture and expressive movement stems from personality. The next chapter will show you what to look for in writing and how to study it.

2 Writing Features

Every child in a class starts with the same copy-book or writing model. Yet somewhere between the mental effort of the eye looking at the book or the blackboard and the manual physical construction of the writing, the influence of the individual self is superimposed on the style. So from very early stages the teacher knows John's writing because it is neat and tidy, Stephen's, because it is all over the place, and Billy's, because it is too big for the page.

All writing starts with a model to copy and the study of handwriting is based on these individual differences—how each person alters and adapts from the original copy-book. These changes from the model are governed by the individual's conscious and unconscious choice and, because personality is dynamic and not static, they will alter with and within the writing as a whole throughout life and according to the physical and mental well-being of the writer.

The British Department of Education and Science confirms that there exists no official ruling as to the method of teaching handwriting in primary schools. There are several styles of copy-book and each has its own adherents.

Print script, sometimes called manuscript, is the model usually used in infant schools, where the letter forms relate as closely as possible to the type in early reading books.

This is Print Script

These letter forms are usually kept as a model until the age of 7 or 8 when a more cursive (running) joining up style is used. The cursive copy-book, called Civil Service or Copper Plate, is used as a model. This style was advocated by Vere Foster, a man who designed his own copy-books some time before World War II:

wait for no man

A copy-book designed by Marion Richardson, a teacher in Birmingham, is also used as a model. It is a careful and more rounded development of print script. This style can be continued through secondary school without the introduction of any cursive joined up writing:

The quick brown fox jumps *

The Italic script, based on the style promoted by the Vatican

Chancery in the fifteenth century, and also called Chancery script, has its devotees, and certainly if the teacher writes in the Italic style herself she is likely to teach it:

Love is a fragrant flower, marriage a tree swept by the wind; but a little girl is a garden filled with sunshine.

These copy-book forms can start with larger proportions but in the main the proportions of the final model are similar. The overall height of the writing is approximately 9mm.

Basically, writing can be divided into three different sections—the movements upwards, away from the body, movements of the small letters along, laterally, and movements downwards towards the body. In the study of handwriting, or graphology, these are called:

U/Z	Upper Zone		3	
M/Z	Middle Zone	*Graphology*	3	9mm
L/Z	Lower Zone		3	

and will be referred to by these terms in the rest of this book.

In this chapter we will see how each individual can alter from the copy model and in the next chapter the psychological implications of these alterations will be discussed. The writer we are talking about should have reached a stage of writing maturity where his attention is focused on the ideas and material he is putting down on paper and not on the manual difficulties of forming his letters. His writing flows along fairly fluently.

1 Size

The first way you can change from the model is in the size of your writing. You can either enlarge or diminish it.

(a) small
(b) average
(c) large

(a) Small *I almost got the whole of that last sentence in one line. had a thicker nibbed pen and had to write large to make it legible. on paper, such a saving!*

(b) Average *my handwriting has a particular weakness in that the m's, n's and u's are not easily distinguishable.*

(c) Large *Ready to be anything of being ever.*

2 Slant

The next way you can alter your writing is in the slant.
(a) left slant
(b) upright
(c) right slant
(d) changes in slant

(a) Left slant

There was an old tramp all tattered and torn, eating the grass at the foot of our lawn. *

(b) Upright

Under a spreading gooseberry bush the village burglar lies. *

(c) Right slant

democracy is the recurring delusion that most of the people are right most of the time. *

(d) Changes in slant

What is wrong with the post war generation? They can have their freedom, but why do they have to use it to develop a cult of ugliness? *

3 Width

You can also alter the width of your writing. Most copy-books start with equal proportions in the M/Z (Middle Zone) letters; the 'n', for example, should be as high as it is wide.
(a) narrow

(b) average
(c) broad

(a) Narrow

" From these [Sequenzi, Corelli, Vivaldi, Albinoni and Frescobaldi] models he [J. S. Bach] acquired the organised clarity combined with elastic freedom which distinguished him from his German forerunners, whose musical utterance had tended either to looseness of thought or extreme rigidity of form. " – "The Music of Bach," by Charles Sanford Terry. *

(c) Broad   The majority of what I have written here is the truth. *

4 Zones

In copy-book writing, all three zones are in equal proportion. You can alter these proportions in numerous ways. Remember these alterations are governed by your own conscious or unconscious choice:

(a) U/Z can be large and M/Z and L/Z small

(b) U/Z and L/Z can be large and M/Z small

(c) L/Z can be large, M/Z average and U/Z small

(d) The writer can stick to the copy-book dimensions in any or all of these

(e) M/Z and L/Z can be large and U/Z small

(f) U/Z and M/Z can be large and L/Z small

(g) M/Z can be large and U/Z and L/Z small

(a) U/Z large, M/Z and L/Z small

Dear Sir,

I wish to be considered

for the position of Branch manager

(b) U/Z and L/Z large, M/Z small

This is being written on Sunday

in the garden, in glorious

(c) L/Z large, M/Z average, U/Z small

Centre, and so this is included on

reverse side of the form.

(d) U/Z, M/Z, L/Z average

Speed and legibility are the essential
characteristics of good handwriting"

(e) M/Z and L/Z large, U/Z small

The knowledge that is got without pains is kept without pleasure.

(f) U/Z and M/Z large, L/Z small

The grass next door may be
greener but it is just as

(g) M/Z large, U/Z and L/Z small

The Mensa intelligence test

5 Regularity

All copy-books give a regular constant shape and form to their letters. Some people cannot control their letter forms, slant or size; the writing can show:
(a) a regular pattern
(b) average conformity
(c) an irregular pattern

(a) Regular pattern

Some six years of working pretty well twenty-four hours a day, seven days a week, three hundred and sixty-five days a year, had left me drained of every ambition and desire except that of spending at least a month in bed, preferably in a padded cell to which neither outcries nor 'incidents' could penetrate. *

(c) Irregular pattern

My writing is notoriously illegible to everyone including my own secretary. *

6 Letters connected or disconnected

Although you may have started with print script copy-book and may not have learned a joined up copy, something inside decides whether you want finally to join your letters or leave them separate, so you can write with:
(a) all letters disconnected
(b) some letters connected and some disconnected
(c) all letters connected

(a) Disconnected

"In an island everything is near, for compressed within it are all the things which are spread out over a nation or a continent, and there *

26

(c) Connected

I don't believe in fairies, ghosts or graphologists. *

7 Form of connection between letters

Copy-books and instructions dictate the way the writer should join his letters together and although everyone strives to emulate the model, again individuality creeps in. You can write with:

(a) angles	(b) arcades	(c) copy-book connections

(d) garlands	(e) threads	(f) mixed connections

Garland writers write 'n's like 'u's; arcade writers write 'u's like 'n's.

(a) Angles

I got to Victoria in time, made East Grinstead in time to start the game promptly at 2:30. *

(b) Arcades

I am not knowledgeable about graphology but I am interested in it, and look forward to reading in "Interim" the findings of this survey. *

(c) Copy-book

The worst moment of an atheist's life is when he feels grateful and has no-one to thank. *

(d) Garlands

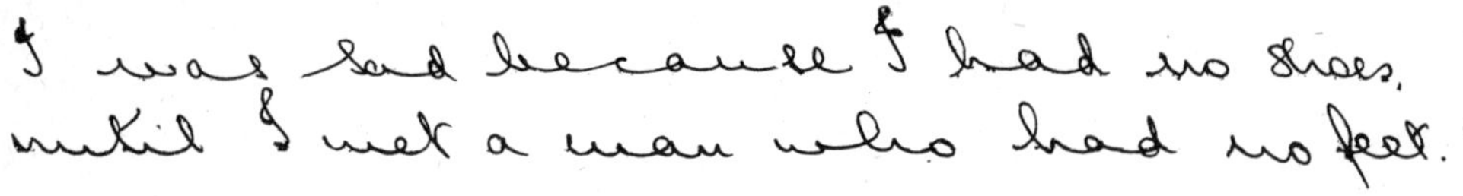
I was sad because I had no shoes, until I met a man who had no feet. *

(e) Threads

(f) Mixed connections

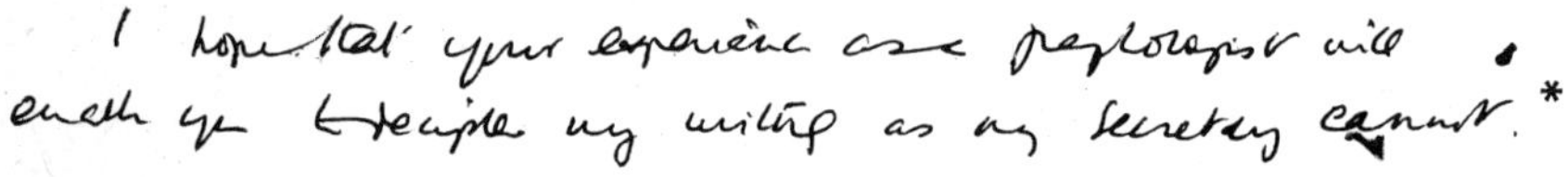
I hope that your experience as a graphologist will enable you to decipher my writing as my secretary cannot. *

8 Pressure

The best way to assess pressure is to see how much impression the writing has made on the back of the paper. If you write on very fine paper and no sign of the writing has come through, you have 'light pressure'. If you write on very thick paper and the pen digs into the paper to the degree that all the writing pattern is visible on the other side, you have 'heavy pressure'. Note if it is:

(a) heavy pressure
(b) medium pressure
(c) light pressure

(a) Heavy pressure

A man's level of being attracts his life. *

(c) Light pressure

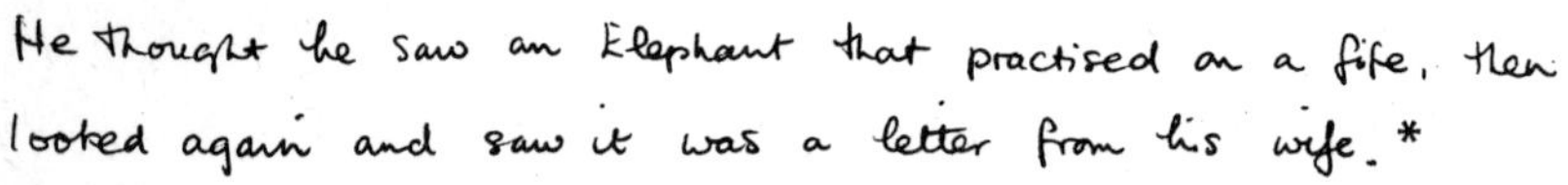
He thought he saw an Elephant that practised on a fife, then looked again and saw it was a letter from his wife. *

9 Stroke

The possible ways of making one single stroke of the pen can run into many millions and the actual magnified stroke of the writing can be one of the most important features. Here we will only concern ourselves as to whether you prefer:
(a) a thin pen and a fine stroke; this is called 'sharp'
(b) a not very thick and not very thin pen
(c) a thick pen and a thick stroke; this is called 'pasty'

(a) Sharp

> 'The moving finger writes, and having writ
> moves on . Nor all thy piety nor wit, shall
> lure it back to cancel half a line, nor
> all thy tears wash out a word of it" *

(c) Pasty

Do not unsaddle the horses; the innkeeper's
rice pudding has been struck by lightning. *

10 Lines

All copy-books give a straight orderly line which progresses steadily across the page. See if in your writing:
(a) lines fall downwards
(b) lines keep straight ahead
(c) lines rise upwards

(a) Lines falling

This is the way I write best that is when I write small,
to you this may also look a mess but I like to think I
can write neatly somtimes. *

(b) Straight lines

There is nothing perhaps in the way of
exhortation and scolding that the ordinary daughter
or son dislikes so much as to be told of her or
his "parent".   (Anthony Trollope, "Lady Anna") *

(c) Lines rising

*Do you remember what became of those wise men who debated "how many fairies can stand on the tip of a pin"? ***

11 Word spacing and line spacing

Copy models give an even spacing between words, some saying that this space should be no greater than that taken up by one letter 'n', and some saying two or two-and-a-half letter 'n's, with more space being allowed after punctuation marks and full stops. They also allow even spaces between lines and no copy-book allows the U/Z of the line below to be written through the L/Z of the line above. You can change from the model in the space you leave between the words; it can be:
(a) wide (leaving space vacant)
(b) average
(c) narrow (filling space)
You can also change the spacing *between* the lines, making it:
(a) wide (leaving space vacant)
(b) average
(c) narrow (sometimes mingling with the line above)

(a) Wide (leaving vacant space)

*Glad to have been of help to the cause of graphological knowledge. ***

(c) Words and lines near together (filling space)

*The sky is blue this morning, amply edged by clouds, harried by a fresh wind which wags the yellow and blue iris wildly, and is clutched at by the tendrils of clematis growing by my window. ***

12 Margins

Although no copy-book gives a guide line as to the margins you should use when putting pen to a blank sheet of paper, there is an aesthetic natural limit of all round margins. Perhaps you:
(a) cling to the left edge of the paper
(b) make a very wide left margin
(c) make a very wide right margin
(d) choose to continue right up to the extreme edge of the paper

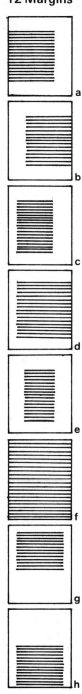

(e) have all round wide margins
(f) have no margins at all
(g) cling to the top of the page
(h) sink to the bottom

Apart from these twelve features, there are a number of other aspects to handwriting such as the speed, the fullness of loops, the 't' crosses and 'i' dots, end strokes, starting strokes and myriads of other small unconscious gestures and movements which no copybook prescribes. Take the whole style; is it simplified or elaborate, natural or artificial?

There are many writings in which unconscious movements and small features such as 't' crosses and 'i' dots, or the lack of them, can be important. The next example shows how the 't' crosses in a writing can visually dominate other aspects.

An analogy can be drawn to the physical appearance of someone's face; in rare cases, a blemish or a beauty spot, a tooth, or the lack of it, can draw the eye and take visual precedence over other important facial features.

Let's make it short *

With all the variables that constitute a writing, people exercise their own choice; they combine to form the individual fabric, so that we can recognize each writing as unique. The overall pattern has a rhythm and harmony of its own. The rhythm can be peaceful and unruffled, flowing, dynamic, strident, monotonous, comfortable, chaotic. It is the sum of the ingredients and components that blend to form a complete picture.

If you want to make an analysis of your own writing, make a larger copy of the chart, Fig. 10 (overleaf). With the twelve features listed on the chart, go back through Chapter 2 and tick in the appropriate boxes in columns X, Y, Z. Then, when you read through Chapter 3 put comments in the space on the right of the chart, as you come to the interpretation of the features which concern your writing. If you find that most of your ticks come in the centre column, Y, they will be more indicative of 'what you are not', since they will show that you fall *between* two extremes.

	Features	X	Y	Z	Comments (see Chapter 3)
1	Size	a	b	c	
2	Slant	a	b	c	
				d	
3	Width	a	b	c	
4	Zones	a		e	
		b	d	f	
		c		g	
5	Regularity	a	b	c	
6	Connected	a	b	c	
7	Form of Connection	a		d	
		b	f	e	
		c			
8	Pressure	a	b	c	
9	Stroke	a	b	c	
10	Lines	a	b	c	
11	Word & Line Spacing	a	b	c	
12	Margins	a	e	b	
		c	f	d	
			g		
			h		
	Total XY&Z				

Figure 10

3 Interpretation
of Writing Features

In the last chapter each feature of writing was carefully considered; in this chapter the psychological implications of these features will be outlined. N.B. NO ONE FEATURE IN HANDWRITING MEANS ANYTHING BY ITSELF—any more than one piece of a jigsaw puzzle makes sense on its own. Each feature has a range of interpretations, which will be highlighted, obscured or deflected by the other features.

Although only three examples are given of writing size, it can be graded through very large, large, average, fairly small, and small, and the strength of the interpretation should be pitched and amplified accordingly. The same applies to slant, which can range between extreme left and extreme right.

It is impossible to cover the whole spectrum of interpretation, positive and negative, which each writing feature can cover. To understand the complexity, imagine a picture of a sunlit scene, with a tree in the centre throwing a shadow that hides part of the picture. One feature of an individual's handwriting can similarly alter the overall interpretation.

1 Size
(a) Small writing
If the writer has an inner desire to make his writing smaller, this is symptomatic of a desire to contract, to concentrate and focus realistically on a small field. It is a sign of introversion and objectivity; it can indicate feelings of inferiority.

The small writer may shun publicity; he is modest, knows humility and does not overstate his case. Where the large writer may need a large house and space for his extravagant parties, the small writer can be quite happy with a small flat to entertain a few close friends.

Small writers tend to have scientific or technical jobs in which they can concentrate their efforts. The age of specialization has produced more small writers, with a different general pattern of writing. Eighty or more odd years ago the pattern was large; people were active and more adventurous; there were plenty of real 'characters' about, and many people were conditioned to go out and seek their fortune in the Empire.

(c) Large writing
If the writer has a desire to enlarge his writing, he has an inner desire to expand, to magnify his focus and extend his field of interest. The other dominant features and pattern of the writing will give an indication as to how and where the ambitions of the writer lie. If his desire to think 'big' is supported by intelligence and a drive outwards into the world, he has all the ingredients for success. There is power in 'mind' and if you do not picture or conceive of

yourself mentally doing great things you most likely will not.

If the writer's desire for 'magnification' is turned in on himself, he can have feelings of superiority, a 'swollen head' or be 'too big for his boots'. He may have an inner need for notoriety, 'holding the stage', having large parties and exaggerating events—there can be an element of childishness in large writers.

Most stars, pop-singers and celebrities enlarge their writing; they enjoy the limelight and being in the public eye. The saddest people are those ambitious people who 'think big' but have not the intelligence, ability for hard work or financial backing to realize their goal. They can feel things are loaded against them.

Most world leaders have large writing; one exception was Mahatma Gandhi. His writing seems to vary in size, but at one time was very small. It is interesting that his method of leadership was to humble himself and, as it were, lead from below.

Fig. 11 shows the writing of Sir Winston Churchill. This is not large writing; but as well as being an outstanding leader, Churchill was also a writer and an artist—a man of many parts. The writing, which is beautifully arranged and spaced on the paper, flows rhythmically along. It is very likely that because he was not pompous or grandiose, but had a natural, unaffected concept of self and an outgoing personality, the British people were able to work with him, and he with them, to make an outstanding partnership.

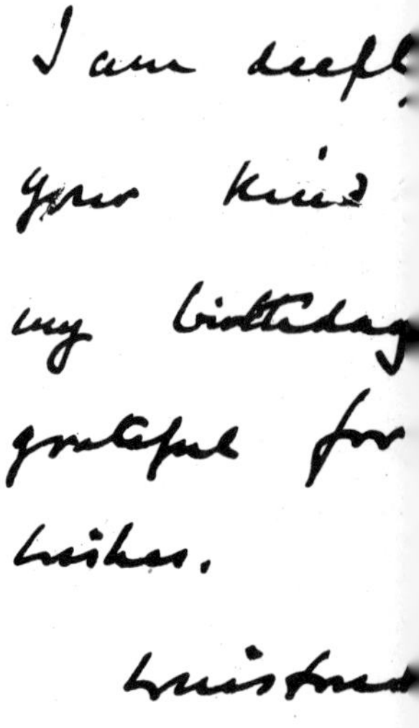

Figure 11

2 Slant

Most copy-books are upright or slant slightly to the right and yet, as indicated in the examples in Chapter 2, personal preference in slant covers a wide angle.

In our western culture we write from left to right and the starting point of every written manuscript is on the left. This is the entrance, the beginning, the place where the message originates. The writing moves away from the writer, away from his body, towards the outside world to its destination, the person to whom he is writing.

As the pen moves across the page, the left becomes the writer's past, the place he has come from, the present is the place he has reached—the centre of the page, perhaps—and the future, to which he will be proceeding, lies ahead. We live in a right-handed world; to understand why this is so, perhaps we should go back to very early times. In the Stone Age the tools that man used were very simple to make. It was easy to chip and sharpen them on either side and there is evidence that as many men used the left hand as the right. However, as technological development in tool making took place, in the Bronze and Iron Ages, tools took longer to make. It became apparent that it would be much simpler to make them specifically for one hand and the right hand emerged as dominant. From the time that tools were made specially for the right hand, it became a matter for the survival of the species that men were right-handed. It became a cultural law and was built into the social code; the left hand became taboo.

34

From the taboo the left became known as inferior. The honoured guest sat on the right hand. According to the dictionary 'right' stands for correct, best, true, just, fair, not mistaken, morally good or desirable.

Hermaphroditic deities are connected with many myths and religions in countries as far apart as Egypt, Mexico and India. (See Figs. 12(a) and (b).) They symbolize duality and unity, the myth of birth and creation, and are probably linked with the Gemini archetype. It is interesting, however, that in these deities the left side of the body is depicted as female and the right side as male. In Fig. 12(a) the left hand holds the lotus flower and the right arm has a coiling snake. The snake is a well-known symbol of masculinity.

(a) Left slant

To return once more to the symbolism of the writing field, people whose writing slopes to the left, example 2(a), show some resistance to the environment which can result in defiance, and in negative and defensive attitudes. They can be contemplative, passive people, liable to stay in their shells and hide their emotions. They have not cut free completely from the past, early experience, origins, home and family ties. They can either have a close affinity with their mother or be dominated in some way by her. The left is a sign of femininity. Left slant writers are often found in jobs connected with history and the past or in research, back-room type jobs.

(b) Upright

Upright writing indicates self-reliance, poise, calm, self-collection, reserve, a neutral attitude, neither 'wholly for' nor 'coldly against', weighing one's words, self-sufficiency. The Queen and Prince Philip both have upright writing. Royalty need to emanate poise and calm. Fig. 13 shows a portrait, the writing and signature of Queen Elizabeth I; the extra large size and embellishments round her signature stress the importance she attached to her public image, which is mirrored in the magnificence of her dress.

(c) Right slant

Right slant shows an involvement with the environment, leaning forward towards others, the future and the common goal, progressiveness, activity, masculinity. The right slant writer wants to communicate with others, is emotionally responsive and demonstrative. He can tend to worry and depend on others, since he sometimes shows a lack of resistance to outside influence.

(d) Changes in slant

If a writing changes in slant in the course of a written passage, the writer will have changing inclinations and changing views, so he will be somewhat unpredictable to himself and others. This sort of writing is often found in young people at puberty when they are unsettled, frequently altering course, trying to 'find themselves'.

ARDANARI ISWARA.

Figures 12(a) and 12(b)

Figure 13

There is evidence that this type of writing in adults can arise from their having parents of different temperaments, who, metaphorically speaking, pull the child unknowingly in different directions. One particularly fluctuating writing was found to belong to a young man who lived in a house where his mother and father were not on speaking terms. His job was to carry messages between the two.

Up to the present time in our western culture, we live predominantly in a man's world; we tend to admire an extroverted, masculine, outgoing type of personality. In the East, where the writing can run from right to left, a more contemplative, passive person is admired.

It is interesting that at one time in history, in the lands bordering on the east of the Mediterranean Sea, there was a writing called Bostrophedon or 'as the ox ploughs', which ran with one line going left to right and the next right to left. It probably originated because it was easier for the scribe or engraver to turn the material as he wrote. This writing came into being at a time of change, when the people were moving from a society dominated by female gods (Astarte was one), to a society dominated by the masculine god, Zeus.

Britain, at the present time, seems to have rather lost its way or its goal for the future; the path ahead has become temporarily obscured. Over the last few years Britain seems to have been trading on the past, selling historic pageantry and past greatness. It is interesting, in view of the symbolism of left and right, past and future, that this moment in history is the first time a woman has been elected as leader of one of Britain's political parties.

3 Width
(a) Narrow
We talk of people being 'narrow-minded', or holding 'narrow views'. If we think of writing as a curtain which is pleated with rufflette—in wide writing it is swinging, pulled free, but in narrow writing it is pulled up tighter; it is restricted but more controlled, and loses its ability to swing freely.

The narrow writer can be well disciplined but he can be restricted and confined; he can have inner inhibitions and fears which cramp his personality. He can be economical and hold on to things so that he becomes mean.

(c) Broad
The dictionary's definition of 'broad' is 'large across'; the desire for lateral expansion is shown in broad writing. We talk of people being 'broad minded', or holding 'broad views'. To 'broadcast' seed is to scatter it freely, not in drills or rows; news is also 'broadcast'. We talk of 'spreading news abroad', which is making news known widely; we talk of 'going abroad'. The meaning of 'abroad' is 'over a wide space, out in the open air'.

The broad writer has an inner desire for expansion laterally—he is uninhibited, likes to have elbow room and spread himself about. If you see someone taking up lots of space in the train, with his legs up, he is likely to be a broad writer. He likes being free and unfettered; he likes to travel and is drawn to the wide world out of doors. He is not confined in person or in conversation. He is purposeful and goal-minded, and on the more negative side he may be rash, obtrusive and somewhat prodigal.

Perhaps now you can see how conflicts build up in a personality. If you have a sample of right slant writing that is narrow, the writer will be active, and involved with other people and the environment, but at the same time he will be shy and inhibited, unable to give full, free expression to his involvement.

Similarly, if you get a left slant writing which is broad, the writer will be very expansive and outgoing and yet can withdraw emotionally and not want close contact with others.

Again, if you have a very large writing which is very narrow, you will have the sort of person who arranges large parties and takes on large enterprises and then, as the time comes near, gets cold feet and inhibitions and tries to cancel them.

4 Zones

When the writer is confronted with a blank sheet of paper, he is symbolically confronted with his own position in space and time, his attitude to himself and to others, the past and the future. To the left lies his childhood and the past, to the right lies the future, work to be done and fellow creatures.

Symbolically, when we think of 'above', we think of the sky and the heavens, infinity, the home of deities. We talk of having 'high aspirations', of 'living up to ideals', of 'lifting up our hands in supplication'.

In earlier times church spires were markedly higher than other buildings; now high-rise blocks reach higher than the spires. This is most noticeable in New York City, where the church spires seem infinitesimal and insignificant beside the towering blocks dedicated to material business.

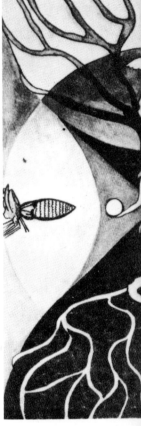

A Tree of Life (from C. J. Jung's *The Philosophical Tree*)

We think of the ground, the earth on which we walk as the here and now, the place where we actually live and move about in our everyday social interactions and contacts. Symbolically, places below the ground have always been connected with mystery, the underworld, from which life springs. Seeds go into the earth, they germinate below ground and come to bloom if conditions are favourable. Trees have roots that grow into the earth to hold them firm. They are foundations which consolidate the position and security of the tree; they give it strength. From below the ground comes the tree's source of nourishment.

The tree has a spreading, vertical shape. Its roots are underground, its trunk is firm and solid and its branches reach up into the sky. Many religions have used the 'Tree of Life' as a potent symbol.

We talk of getting down to business, being down to the ground,

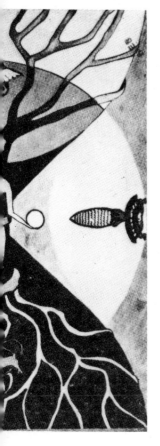

undertaking, underclothes, being a bit earthy. We talk of Mother Earth. When people die, they return to the earth. Symbolically they can be reborn, in the way that the leaves of the tree die in the autumn and fall, and yet in the spring come to life again in new shoots.

What implications has this for handwriting? If you look back to Chapter 2 you will see a number of the possible permutations of zonal proportion. The zones of the writing can be compared to a tree; the U/Z with the branches, the M/Z with the trunk and the L/Z with the roots.

(a) U/Z large, M/Z and L/Z small
Here we have someone who strives and has high aspirations and desires, but has little social self-confidence or interest in everyday social life. He has no solid roots or foundations to his personality. While he may achieve a great deal because he is motivated to strive, he lacks balance and consolidation, and his endeavours may not be substantiated in reality. If the capital letters are very high we can have a person with his head in the air, who does not sense where he is going; he is not 'down to earth'.

(b) U/Z and L/Z large, M/Z small
Here we have striving and aspirations supported by physical stamina, a materialistic outlook, and good business sense, but there lacks an inner centre to sustain the personality. This person can be dissatisfied with what he has achieved, always looking for new experiences and enterprises. He can escape from the reality of everyday into activity and sometimes bites off more than he can chew.

(c) U/Z small, M/Z average, L/Z large
This type of writer has a strong material and instinctive drive; he is very down to earth and earthy. His bias, depending on the stroke of the writing, is sex or money. He has little other motivation, his aspirations are limited and he has an average investment in his everyday social life.

(d) Copy-book dimensions
The writer that sticks to the copy-book proportions has a balanced outlook; he has no exaggerated bias. The truly happy person has an individual and yet balanced personality, with inner harmony. The more out of balance and extreme a personality becomes the more talented the writer may be in unusual directions.

(e) M/Z and L/Z large, U/Z small
This writer has strong social self-confidence, social involvement, strong material and instinctive drive, and little aspiration upwards. If the L/Z loop is over long (example (a)), this can indicate compensation for some disturbance in his love life. If it is extended in a large loop (example (b)), it can be that he dreams of making money

example (a)

example (b)

or of sexual adventures. If it is very long and open, like a scoop (example (c)), it can be that he is in touch with the underworld, mystery, and the unconscious mind, and he can scoop up weird ideas and scenarios.

(f) U/Z and M/Z large, L/Z small

Here we have a writer with high ambitions and good self-confidence, but his personality has no deep roots. If the L/Z strokes are extremely short, it can mean repression of instinct; this could, depending on the rest of the writing (the slant, the stroke, and the pressure), have an explosive possibility. The writing of Neville Heath, the sex murderer, showed a very stunted L/Z with a pasty, muddy stroke to the writing.

(g) M/Z large, U/Z and L/Z small

Where the dominant aspect of the writing is M/Z we get a personality who lives in the here and now; gossip, social involvement and grandeur being the central theme of his life. He does not have high aspirations, nor is he motivated towards making money. The danger to this sort of writer is boredom and confinement in a self-centred world. This is a feminine tendency; large M/Z writers have social self-confidence and feel at home in social gatherings. Most men have small M/Z writing which reflects their dislike of parties and other social events.

5 Regularity and Irregularity
(a) Regular pattern

The dictionary meaning of 'regular' is 'orderly, conforming to a rule, uniform, symmetrical, steady, unvarying'. We talk of being 'as regular as clock-work', of 'regular soldiers' or of someone being a 'regular civil servant'. There is a permanency about it. See example 5(a) of regular writing. It is steady and disciplined and has symmetry, so we would expect the regular writer to be a well-disciplined person, who has control of his impulses and energies. A sense of duty dominates his feelings; he is controlled and likes order. He is predictable and can be relied upon to behave in an orderly manner.

More negatively, he can lack verve, excitability, versatility and the capacity to change, so he can be monotonous and rather dull. He can live under a compulsion that things have to be 'to order' in a disciplined routine. He can become a victim of a treadmill of work that he feels obliged to complete, or a schedule to fill, rather like a hamster on its wheel. Who has not heard of the serving officer whose home was 'run' like a ship or a command?

(c) Irregular pattern

Once more we have the opposite tendency in writing, which will have an opposing implication in the personality. The dictionary says for irregularity, 'not uniform' and we can take this as good advice. It is not a good idea for the irregular writer to go into the army.

He will be in trouble from the beginning. We have all heard of 'irregular behaviour'. The irregular writer can be disorderly, lack steadiness and self-discipline, and be unsure of his plans; he loves variety and change.

Some people might say he should join the army; 'it will knock him into shape'. It might for a few people, but others will feel imprisoned and trapped, and their excitability and varying and changing inclinations, instead of working for them, will be a heavy liability.

Irregular writers can be emotional, impressionable people who can work from chaos and powerful impulses, but not from an ordinary sense of duty. They are never dull or entirely predictable; at their worst they can be hectic, undirected, unsettled and all over the place. Some great creative geniuses have been irregular writers.

Young people's writing in adolescence can go through a patch of irregularity, when they are in a process of personal change and finding their foothold in the world.

6 Connection and disconnection
(a) Disconnected

'Disconnect' means 'sever connections between, separate, disjoin'. A disconnected writer's thoughts are disjoined; he can have brilliant, unique thoughts and many ideas that emerge singly as inspirations. He is attracted to items and detail, not to the 'whole'. He can be illogical and whimsical, and find it difficult to make friends because he does not see connections and relations.

If he reads a book, it may be one small remark or detail of it that holds his imagination, rather than the entire book. One wife of a disconnected writer summed up this type of mind very well when she said, 'He does not take in the whole crowd at a party, but he will notice a small ladder in one lady's tights'. He is the sort of heartbreaking boss who does not notice all you have accomplished but will notice one minute flaw in the whole achievement.

Disconnected writers do not have a strong chain of thought to garrison and protect them from the unconscious mind and from the mysterious. If their writing has a long L/Z (example 6(a)), they can be people who know intuitive depths, feel ghosts, and have an uncanny 'sense' for the unknown. They are the designers and abstract painters who can conceive and dream up the bizarre and the extraordinary; theirs is a whole world which is 'shut' to and scoffed at by the connected writer. Note the written content of example 6(c).

(c) Connected

Conversely, 'to connect' means 'to join together, link, show relationships between, associate, follow logically'. If a writer joins all his letters together and links them all, he has a strong 'chain' which can give strength and integration to his personality. His thoughts are associated one with another. He does not have a grasshopper mind which jumps and flits from one thought to

Figure 5 (overleaf): In Egyptian hieroglyphics, the name of the god Osiris is a rebus of an eye, a throne and a sceptre (see p. 14)

another. There is a good flow to his conversation; one thing leads constructively to the next.

The connected writer has a great capacity for getting things done because he sees the sequence and logical order in which to do them. He can mix easily and associate with other people because he sees and understands relationships. The chain of his thoughts can provide a solid barrier to ideas and inspirations, preventing them from emerging individually from his unconscious mind. Very connected writers can be 'blind' to insight and to how they are affecting others.

7 Connection between letters
(a) Angles
As explained in Chapter 2, people show personal preference in the way they connect each letter together. Some handwriting analysts call this their 'personal form of adjustment'. Several different types of connection can appear in one writing.

Looking at the example on p. 27, 'angles' give a feeling of durability and sharpness; like rocks and crags, they are definite, with no vagueness or softness; like an iron fence, they are rigid with no pliability. There is no 'flow' with angles, they can hinder the natural relaxed course of the writing by introducing a stiffness. Therefore we can expect the angular writer to be firm, strong-minded, hard, uncompromising, tense, and tending to lack the ability to 'feel'.

(b) Arcades
Another way you can connect your letters is with 'arcades'. The dictionary says an 'arcade' is a 'covered avenue, or a covered walk, lined with shops, not open to the sky'. The arcade is a gesture of covering over; something of the arcade is suggested in the formal human gesture of bowing.

We would expect the arcade writer to be formal and to screen over his thoughts. He can be difficult to influence; he likes to take his own council and knows his own business. He does not want the 'covered walk', which is his own, open to others. Symbolically, the arcade is an umbrella or a sentry box, which protects the writer from the rain and the snow, but does not let the sunshine in. High, arched arcades are often found in the writing of sculptors, artists and connoisseurs interested in the moulding of shape and form. Notice in example 7(b), 'u's are written like 'n's.

(c) Copy-book connection
Some people stick to the copy-book connections that they were taught. This can show a lack of innovation and originality, 'taking the conventional line', sticking to preconceived ideas; it can also indicate someone with self-discipline who can take orders and be relied on to carry out instructions to the letter. Or, it can be that the person has adopted a disguise, or 'cloak of conventionality'.

(d) Garlands

The garland is the opposite of the arcade; it is an open receptive gesture. Writing garlands gives a free and easy, natural feeling. If you approach a wild animal with your hand cupped and open it will stay for a while, but if you approach with the palm downwards and arched it will steal away.

Where the arcade writer was protected, the garland writer is vulnerable; this is an open gesture, open for the rain to come into, but also to receive the warm sun. A garland writer can be amiable, receptive, kind, but sometimes gullible. The garland can resemble a waste paper basket and its writer can be receptive to other people's rubbish. If the garland is more like a high, supported cup (example (a)) it can hold bitter resentment and depressive feelings. The shallow garland (example (b)) is a fluent, flexible, non-aggressive movement, showing kindness and unaffected sympathy. Notice example 1(b), 'average size'. He is a garland writer and comments on the fact that his 'm's and 'n's look like 'u's.

uul

example (a)

example (b)

(e) Thread

The thread writer is the opposite of the angular writer. Where angles can show considerable tension and control, thread writing can show too much release and lack of control. The angular writer shows a firm, well defined trace, he stands for something; the thread is formless and elastic, giving no certain trail.

Angles show a backbone to personality; the thread writer appears to be spineless. He can be eternally insecure and uncertain of himself, avoiding decisions, being highly versatile and supple, gliding by, avoiding resistance, bending and swaying as the wind blows.

Threads can suddenly appear in the words of overworked people; when they are under strain they find they are having difficulty making decisions. When this happens they should take a rest. Writing can provide strong evidence of strain and people under strain take more notice when they can actually be shown visual evidence.

(f) Mixed connections

The writer of 'mixed connections' will show variability and some of the qualities of each type of connection.

8 Pressure

Pressure is difficult to assess because it can depend on the type of pen or ball-point used and on the writing surface. Pressure can be general, patchy, lateral, etc. Here we are concerned only with heavy pressure and light pressure. In the last chapter we discussed how to judge pressure.

A person who feels deeply will make a heavy mark with his pen. We talk about 'putting pressure on people' and about 'pressure building up'; by this we usually mean mental, not physical

Overleaf: A detail from a Mixtec pictorial chronicle (c. 1519). It reads from right to left, and people and locations are defined by rebus signs

pressure. In writing, heavy pressure is indicative of psychic energy or force which is not predominantly physical.

One mother brought the writing of her son, which was on an airmail letter form. There was no sign of writing on the other side of the paper, showing very light pressure. She described her son, who was eighteen years old, as 'all brawn and no brain'. We have to think of writing as 'brain writing' and not, in truth, 'handwriting'; the force that directs it comes from the brain—the hand is merely carrying out the messages it receives.

(a) Heavy pressure
Overall heavy pressure can mean strong reserves of energy, vitality, vigour, 'feeling things deeply'. If the writing flows dynamically and is supported by heavy pressure, the writer is capable of achieving a great deal. If the rest of the writing pattern is cramped, upright and regular, the energy and vigour may be trapped without outlet and so strong tension builds up in the personality; 'a heavy hand and a heavy heart'.

(c) Light pressure
These writers hate noise and violence; they have 'fine' feelings and can be sensitive, perceptive and tender. They can lack strong reserves of energy and vitality; they tire easily and they can lack determination and stamina. They can skate over the surface of life without digging into it or getting involved in things deeply.

9 Writing stroke
The character of the stroke of writing is a most important factor; when magnified it can look alive, springy, integrated—or dead, lifeless, disintegrated and amorphous. It can be fragmented, brittle, watery, diluted, blotched, oily, rich, torpid, muddy, dirty, clean, crystal clear, fine, or sharp. It radiates and portrays the life force of the writer. Here we will concern ourselves only with two aspects of stroke—thick writing, which handwriting analysts call 'pasty', and thin, fine writing, which is usually known as 'sharp'.

(a) Sharp writing
The sharp writer will prefer a narrow, fine nib. With an upright angle of the pen and a thin nib, the sharp writer is etching the surface rather than stroking it, with an incisive, clearly cut trace.

For the sharp writer things are clear cut, not indulged in, but critically thought out. We talk of people being as 'sharp as a needle'. There can be a critical, cold severity in sharp writers. They can have keen, acute, penetrating brains and rapier-like tongues. Their interests can be predominantly intellectual and spiritual. Priests and nuns dedicated to the service of others often have 'fine writing', it can be associated with a puritan streak, asceticism, lack of sensuality and inability to enjoy life.

(c) Pasty writing

The pasty writer, given the freedom, will choose a thick nib or a felt pen which will give a thick brush-like stroke to the writing; usually this type of stroke has little pressure and the upstrokes and downstrokes are universally thick. Of course people can borrow pens and ball-point pens and this makes it more difficult to assess how pasty a writing is. In all interpretations it is important to remember that no one aspect in writing has overriding implications on its own. With practice one gets to know how features can relate—what is 'right' for a certain pattern of writing and what is significant because it does not 'fit in'.

Pastiness is produced with a long hold of the pen; the pen forms a very acute angle with the paper (example (a)). In a sharp writing the pen is held tightly and closer to the nib, with an upright angle (example (b)), reducing the surface of the nib that touches the paper.

example (a)

example (b)

10 Rising and falling lines
(a) Falling lines

We talk of being 'dragged down', of 'spirits falling'; of being 'down and out'. We say things are 'getting us down', and we are 'ready to drop'. Falling lines represent and exemplify these feelings.

Pessimism and optimism can be fluctuating tendencies and the same writer can find his lines of writing rising one day and falling the next, according to his moods and state of energy. However, there are, as well, eternal pessimists and eternal optimists.

Ill-health can produce falling lines and falling words in writing and so can general fatigue or depression. If the situation is serious and deeply-rooted there are usually other signs of ill-health in the writing such as a tremor, breaks or patchiness in the stroke and pressure.

(c) Rising lines

The writer whose lines rise up the page shows optimism and elation. We talk of being 'lifted up with joy' and 'rising to the occasion', and of 'rising spirits'. Rising notes in music tend to be more elating than notes going down the scale.

There is also an irrepressibility about things which rise. You cannot keep them down. Fig. 14 is the writing of the Rt. Hon. Anthony Wedgwood Benn. He has been heard to say 'I am fired with optimism'.

11 Spacing of words and lines

Naturalists and others interested in observing wild animals have noticed that when they approach within a certain distance an animal will turn tail and fly. W. Hediger's term for this is 'flight distance'. The antelope will flee when someone approaching is five hundred yards away, and the wall lizard when they are six feet away.

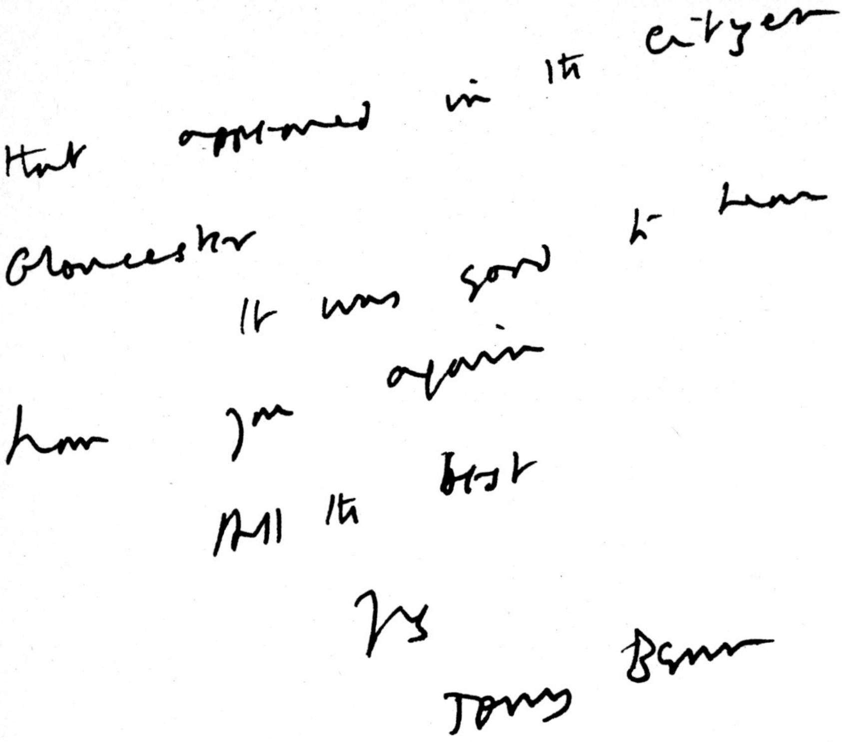

That appeared in its entry[?]
Gloucester
It was good to have
[?] you again
All the best
Yrs
Tony Benn

Figure 14

'Critical distance' is the distance at which an animal does not think it has time to escape and will turn to attack. If a cat is far enough away when a dog starts to chase it, it will bolt up the nearest tree, but if it is too late for escape it will turn and face the enemy, arching its back, to look as large as possible; usually when this happens the dog retires in a gauche manner.

Some species of animals are called 'contact' species—they need to huddle close together and require mass physical contact. The pig, the hippopotamus, and the walrus are called contact species. The dog, the cat, and the horse are not 'contact' species. Man is not a contact species, but he is a social species. He appears to have an individually defined area that surrounds him at any time which is his own 'personal distance'; as well as this he needs to have contact with a social group. The following postscript to the poem 'Prologue: The Birth of Architecture' by W. H. Auden explains the situation well:

> Some thirty inches from my nose,
> The frontier of my Person goes,
> And all the untilled air between
> Is private 'pagus' or demesne,
> Stranger, unless with bedroom eyes
> I beckon you to fraternize,
> Beware of rudely crossing it;
> I have no gun but I can spit.

In his book *The Hidden Dimension,* Edward T. Hall evaluates 'personal distances' in man. Firstly there is the 'intimate distance, close phase'; this is the distance of love-making, wrestling, comforting and protecting. Then there is 'intimate distance, far phase'—a distance of six to eight inches. This can bring physical discomfort in some people; if, for example, a stranger puts his face too close, it tends to make people nervous.

'Personal distance, close phase' is about one and a half feet to two and a half feet; at this distance one can hold or grasp the other person. 'Personal distance, far phase' is two and a half to four feet—having or keeping someone 'at arm's length'.

Then there is 'social distance' which is four to twelve feet, and 'public distance'—some twenty-five feet or more. Thirty feet is the usual distance that is set around important public figures; we have all heard of 'keeping our distance' and 'knowing our place'.

In the business world and the civil service, people tend to have larger offices and desks, and more space, the higher up in the hierarchy they rise. Man, as a species, has a strong hierarchical structure, so the person coming into the large office is more impressed, apprehensive and in awe. The more space there is around you the less familiar and comforting the situation becomes.

—Now, you may well say, what has all this to do with handwriting? The word spacing in writing appears to be an unconscious process, whereas the line spacing is more consciously selected. If you try writing with your eyes shut you will not be so worried about the word spacing, but the inability to see the lines will be upsetting.

John Dumpleton, in his book on handwriting, when talking about spacing between words says, 'One of the chief faults of most handwriting is the excessive spacing between words, and it is one of the most difficult habits to break'. This is hardly surprising.

(a) Wide word spacing, leaving space vacant

Example 11(a) shows wide spaces between words. These writers have a more marked sense of personal distance. There is something exclusive about them; they want to keep their distance. They can have clear, lucid minds but they can also be 'stand-offish' and very selective in their choice of close friends. They do not like living cheek by jowl and they do not like people breathing down their necks or having people push their faces right at them in the way some overpowering people do. Because of this strong sense of keeping personal distance, wide spaces can mean a self-imposed loneliness and lead to isolation.

Fig. 15 shows the writing of the Rt. Rev. Trevor Huddleston; notice how beautifully it is arranged on the paper. Clean, clear cut, concise and simplified, it indicates a high standard—an intellectual writing. Notice also how space is left vacant, showing he is an exclusive and rather isolated person who likes to keep his personal distance. The regularity of his writing shows considerable self-discipline. That it is so small confirms his genuine and sincere personal identification with the 'underdog'.

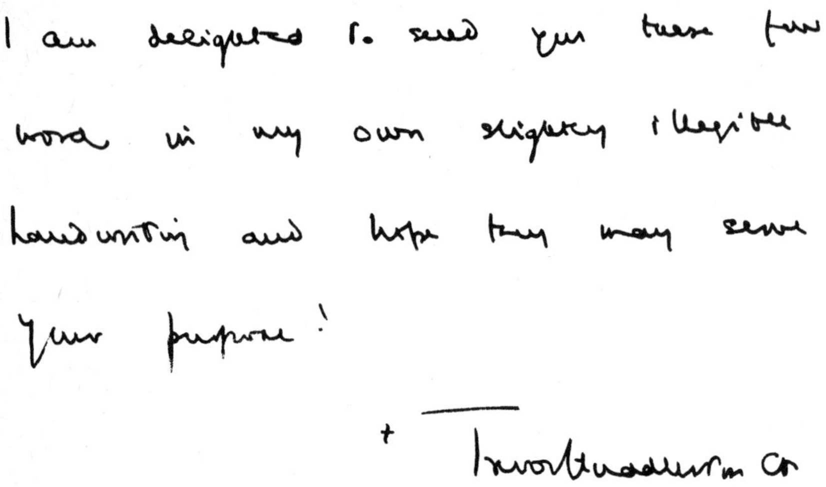

Figure 15

(c) Narrow word spacing, filling space
Here we have someone who has a very close sense of personal distance. There is strong reason to suggest that different nationalities have differing values of personal distance. The English, for example, have a name for being rather remote and cold. Most warmer-blooded more contact-minded foreigners seem to grasp the hand warmly and invade the 'thirty inches from one's nose' at the drop of a hat.

If there are very small spaces between words then the writer prefers company and crowds; he wants to abolish distance and seek close contact, and he likes mixing indiscriminately.

(a) Wide line spacing, leaving space vacant
The writer with wide line spacing shows a capacity for organizing spatially; his thinking is clear and well defined. He likes keeping distance and arrangement in his thoughts.

(c) Narrow line spacing, mingling, filling space
When the writer makes his line spacing too narrow and the loops of one line intermingle with the loops of the next, he tends to lack the capacity for clear, well-defined, organized thinking. He shows an inability to keep distance and arrangement in his thoughts, which can jostle and overlap, confusing and muddling him. He shows a lack of respect for boundaries and an inability to control his impulses.

People who use narrow word spacing and narrow line spacing have a desire to fill and crowd space. If you have them staying with you they seem to 'fill the environment' and 'take it out of you'. Those who use wide word spacing and wide line spacing have an inner desire to leave space vacant; their personalities tend to feel 'lighter', they are not so tiring because they do not 'press' on one.

12 Margins

We have been talking about the spatial arrangement of writing and the word and line spacing. Now we will look into the way the writer fills space or leaves it vacant in the margins; different aspects of this were explained in Chapter 2.

(a) and (b) Left margin

To go back to the symbolism in the left or right slant of writing, the left is the place where we make our entrance. If we start right at the edge of the paper, we are making our entrance naively, with no claims to background lavishness; we are being economical with space and clinging to the door. Children tend to make no margins on the left.

If we are swimming or skating, clinging to the edge implies that we have not fully developed the self-confidence to push off towards the unfilled space in the middle, where we must swim unsupported or try to stand on our own two legs.

We can assume that the writer who makes no left margin at all (example 12(a)) can be economical and makes no pretensions. In example 1(a) the writer uses no margins and mentions the fact that this economizes on paper. He clings to the past, or has no inner need to push off from it.

Conversely, the writer who makes a large left margin (example 12(b)) has an inner need to display his own good cultural background; he has detached himself from the edge. This can be a sign of putting on a show and living on a grand scale. It can also be a sign of cutting off, for some reason, of getting away from oneself, or wanting to get away from the past, and therefore putting 'distance' between it and the present.

(c) and (d) Right margin

If the writer stops before reaching the right hand edge of the paper and leaves a large right margin (example 12(c)), he is leaving space vacant; this can spring from an aesthetic sense of arrangement, but it can also come from an inner fear of the future and the environment and an impulse to back away from rather than face up to things and 'competing'.

If, on the other hand, the writer rushes headlong to the right hand edge of the page (example 12(d)), he may have little aesthetic sense about spatial arrangement, but he also has no inhibitions or reserves about facing up to the future; he has an active involvement with the environment.

(e) Wide margins on all sides

When the written content of a message is placed centrally on the page and the margins on all sides are wide, aesthetically chosen, and in balance, the writing appears to be 'framed' extravagantly by the space left vacant round it (example 12(e)). The writer wants to push off from the past but he is afraid of facing up to the future. He desires exclusion and is exclusive.

One well-known artist who 'uses space' in writing like this, has an area around his house where no strangers are allowed; papers, milk, post, etc. have to be left outside the wall of the garden, where suitable boxes are provided. Friends are also not allowed 'inside' unless they have been asked or have informed him of their intended visit. This form of 'framed' spacing seems to go hand in hand with a sensitive, artistic perception and restraint.

There is some printed note-paper available nowadays which has a coloured line bordering it all the way round, about ten or thirteen millimetres in from the edge of the paper. It can be in any colour, according to the chosen headings and design. Black is frequently chosen. This type of paper was commonly used in Victorian times when there had been a death in the family and the writer was 'in mourning'. Fig 16(a) is an example. The edged note-paper reappearing now as a personal choice, in everyday use, must show an unconscious need for some form of protection. With the edging, the message and the writer seem safer; the line all round gives security and 'centres' and 'sets off' the correspondence.

(f) No margins
The writer who leaves no margins at all, example 12(f), or the writer who does leave a small margin and then fills it up afterwards with extra bits (sometimes even turning the letter upside down and writing his last notes above the address), wants space to be filled in at all costs; there is no exclusiveness. This writer shows 'want of artistic sensitivity'. He wants to hold on to the past and at the same time face up to the future and what it has in store. He can be unceremonious and invade other people's 'personal space'. He can also be economical and thrifty.

In the old days this thriftiness was carried to extremes; when the writer had finished writing one way he sometimes turned the paper sideways and wrote the other way. (See Fig. 16(b).)

(g) Narrow upper margin
Not leaving space vacant at the top, like not leaving distance from your superior or someone who is 'higher up', can show a lack of formality and respect. This narrow top margin is fairly common in the writing of young people today. It can also show high hopes and desire to stay at the 'top'.

(h) Large upper margin
The writer who leaves a large upper margin shows respect and leaves or feels distance between himself and those at the top. It can mean pessimism. The writer may feel that he has not been able to live up to high expectations, or that he is well 'below' where he should be.

Having read to the end of this chapter, you should have a series of comments on the right of your chart, Fig. 10. You should also have a collection of ticks in the columns X, Y, Z. You may find, on looking through the comments that there are a lot of contradic-

Figure 9: Thoth, the Ibis-headed god of the Nile, legendary inventor of Egyptian writing (see p. 17)

Figures 16(a) and right, 16(b)*

tions. Personality can be made up of conflicts and contradictions; it is rather like an old-fashioned tent with many guy ropes pulling in different directions; by their pull they integrate the firmness of the whole structure.

On the chart, column X contains all the headings which are basically signs of 'tightening' and all the ones that fall in column Z are signs of 'loosening'. Those in column Y form a central balance. Add up how many ticks you have in each column and record the total.

If, on adding up the ticks, you have more in column X ('tightening'), your 'tent' or personality is too tightly pulled together; you should take up hobbies and other pursuits to try to release tension. If, on the other hand, you have more in column Z ('loosening'), you should try to pull yourself together, exert more self-discipline and take up pursuits involving 'control'.

Please do not now think that you are an expert handwriting analyst! This chapter has only scratched the surface in order to reveal what a lot there is to discover in handwriting.

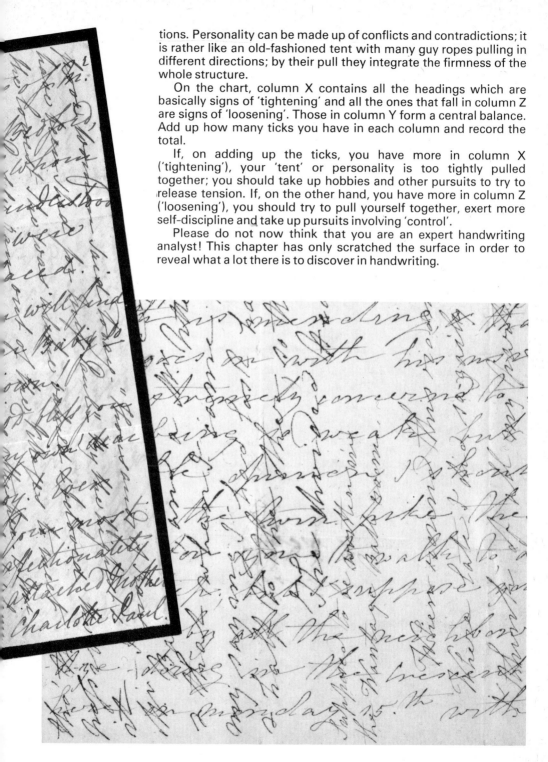

	Features	X	Y	Z	Comments (see Chapter 3)
1	Size	a ✓	b	c	realistic concentration on a small field, introversion, modesty.
2	Slant	a ✓	b	c	resistant, on the defensive
				d	defiant.
3	Width	a	b ✓	c	
4	Zones	a ✓		e	(this chart does not cover all possibilities for Zones. In this instance all 3 zones are small).
		b	d	f	
		c		g	
5	Regularity	a ✓	b	c	good self-discipline, sense of duty.
6	Connected	a	b	c ✓	gets things done, sees things through.
7	Form of Connection	a ✓		d	firm, strong-minded uncompromising.
		b	f	e	
		c			
8	Pressure	a	b ✓	c	
9	Stroke	a	b ✓	c	
10	Lines	a	b ✓	c	purposeful, moves straight ahead.
11	Word & Line Spacing	a	b ✓	c	clear, well-defined orderly thinking.
12	Margins	a	e	b	can stand on his own feet and face up to the future.
		c	f	d ✓	
			g		
			h		
	Total XY&Z	5	5	2	Too much "tension" insufficient "release"

so slow in thanking you that I was caught by the postal strike, and then I forgot and have only just remembered. But I enjoyed myself very much, and it was very kind of you to ask me.

This 21-year-old student's writing shows too much tension—see chart opposite

The knowledge that is got without pains is kept without pleasure. (I can't refrain from completing this quotation:) The struggling for knowledge hath a pleasure in it like that of wrestling with a fine woman.

large middle and lower zone—but carefully constructed style may conceal other factors

'Whatever his weight in pounds shillings + ounces he always seems bigger because of his bounces.'

left-handed or right-handed?

My writing is notoriously illegible. everyone is closing my arm severity.

forceful, adventurous type—but shows impatience with routine—would make a good politician?

It's necessary to keep an equilibrium between

...precise, able—but why so disconnected?
Somewhat emotionally remote

4 The Image of Self

While the signature represents the self to the outside world and to other people, there is another aspect of 'self' in writing—the personal pronoun 'I'. In the English language this 'ego sign' or 'I' is a single letter, which lends itself to individual adaptation and unusual formation. When the personal pronoun is 'Ich' or 'Je', personal design is not as easy. The signature is a more conscious outward emblem than the 'I'. In early Egyptian hieroglyphics the picture of an eye stood for 'eye' and 'I' (the inner eye?).

The personal symbolism of the 'I' can be quite unconscious. When someone is presented with a large page of 'I's and asked to identify his own, quite frequently, if he has a natural and uncomplicated conception of 'self', he has no idea how he makes his 'I' and says he would be quite unable to identify it. The larger and more ornate the 'I', the more readily it can be identified.

It is fairly common for people to use two forms of 'I', one for their entrance and one to use when they have become acclimatized to the conditions prevailing. This has been noticed in the writing of titled people who will make their entrance as someone of consequence and then, when they feel they have played this part, and done justice to it, they will simplify the 'I' and be themselves. (See Fig. 17(a).) Two forms of 'I' can also be found in the writing of transvestites and other people who manifest two different aspects of self.

There are numerous, elaborate and weird designs for the personal pronoun; only by knowing the writer and unravelling the enigma of this 'self image' can the truth of the symbolism be uncovered. If the writer can find out when he adopted an unusual form of 'I', he can usually associate this with events or pressures at the time, which can frequently trigger off memories of associated events from very early in his life.

In all unnatural unconscious movements in writing which give evidence of complexes, obstructing or hindering the flow of the personality, this form of detective work can give relief. If you try to discipline the person and make him consciously alter writing movements, they will appear mysteriously somewhere else in his writing. You cannot force people to be what they are not, without damaging the natural spontaneousness of their personality and forcing them to wear a mask or a partial disguise.

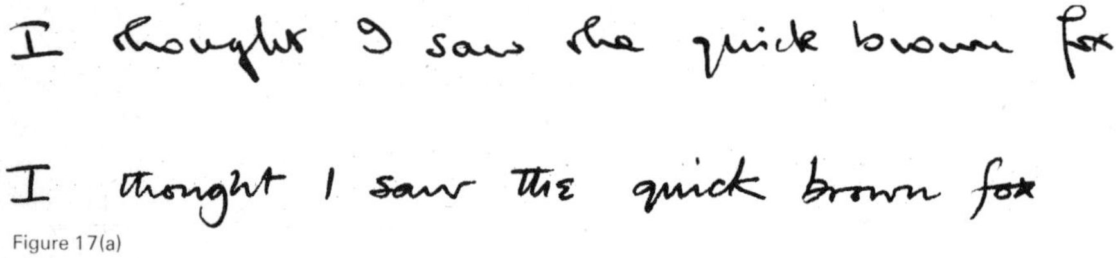

I thought I saw the quick brown fox

I thought I saw the quick brown fox

Figure 17(a)

In a recent survey of 2,000 Mensa members (Mensa is a society which requires its members to have an I.Q. of 148 or over) participants were asked to write what appeared to be an idiotic sentence, 'I thought I saw the quick brown fox jumping over the lazy doggy, but I looked again and saw that it was becoming very foggy.' The reason for the selection of this sentence was that it contained three capital 'I's as well as all the letters of the alphabet. Fig. 17(b) shows six different forms of the capital 'I', and shows, as a percentage, the form preferred by various groups.

Ego Symbol—Forms of the capital 'I'							
	1	2	3	4	5	6	Others
	l	*I*	*ꝯ*	*q*	*ꞡ*	*ꝺ*	
All writings in the survey	33	12	21	4	17	3	10
Males	28	13	23	5	17	3	11
Females	47	8	18	3	17	1	6
Married	30	11	21	5	21	3	9
Single	37	12	23	4	13	2	10
Single and over the average age of marrying	26	12	22	5	20	3	12
Grammar school	26	13	26	5	18	3	9
Public school	56	11	11	2	10	2	8
Left handed	33	25	15	5	12	3	7
Right handed	34	10	22	4	17	3	10

Figure 17(b)

Group (1) A single writing stroke. One finger held up indicates one person, and one single stroke was the most popular form of 'I' in the survey. This is a simplified, unaffected form; it is the model used in the Marion Richardson copy-book as well as in 'print script' and some italic scripts. This form of 'I' had a strong feminine/public school bias, as shown in the figures of the survey.

Group (2) The form of 'I' which has a 'hat' and a 'pedestal' is the copy-book form of some italic scripts. In the survey, it had a masculine bias and was markedly preferred by left-handed people. If you ask someone who uses this form of 'I' why they use it, in-

61

stead of a single stroke, they usually say or imply that a single stroke is 'not enough'. They feel an inner need for more personal emphasis in their 'ego'.

Figure 48 (right): 'my family' painted by Paul, aged 7 (see p. 83)

Group (3) This is the copy-book form of 'I' for ordinary cursive, 'civil service' type writing. It has an angular, pointed formation in the U/Z.

Group (4), (5) and (6) These are other personal adaptations, but with circular formations.

Group (7) Other variations of the 'ego symbol' showed an astonishing variety.

The American Palmer copy-book (Fig. 18), gives a form of capital 'I' which is conventional in America but rare in Britain. Only three people in the survey used it and they had all learned to write in America.

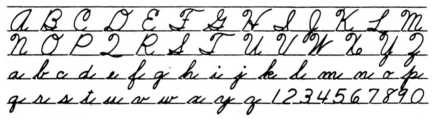

Figure 18*

Another unusual way of writing the 'I' is to start at the base line and write from bottom to top. Three people in the survey chose this way of making their 'I'. It is hard to be sure that someone has inverted the 'I' unless you actually see him do it, or it is connected on to the next word, as it is in Fig. 19. This type of 'I' is the reverse of any known copy-book or model.

If something inside you wishes to oppose conventional forms, and this opposition shows up in the way you see yourself when you write, then it must go very deep. So one can expect writers of the reversed 'I' to do the opposite of what is expected and to be 'different'. They can have original, brilliant minds, even genius; the rest of their writing can show the direction, felicitous or disastrous, in which their 'difference' leads them. This kind of 'I' may also be a

Figure 19

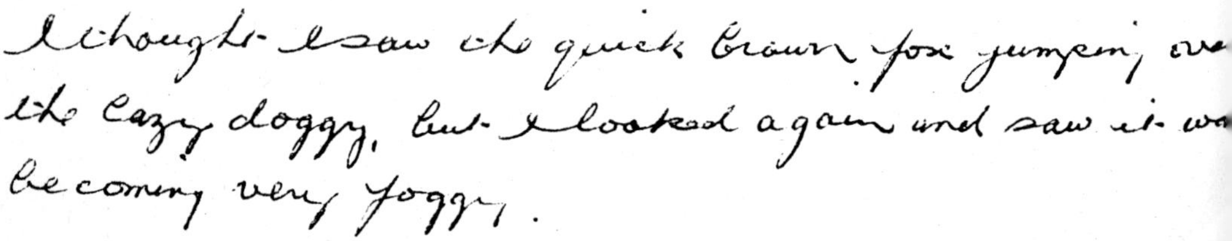

Paul

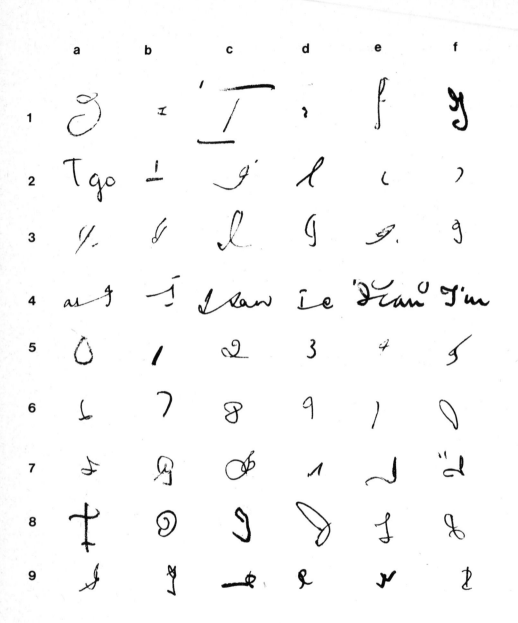

Figure 20

'fossil' reminder of some iconoclastic tendencies in early life. Fig. 20 shows fifty-four different personal pronoun 'I's, all taken from correspondence with the author.

Starting with 1(a) and 1(c) we have ego symbols that use up space both vertically and horizontally; the writers have an inflated

Figures 21 (top) and 22

idea of 'self'. Sample 1(c) is from the writing of a model, used to being in the limelight and holding the stage. On the other hand, 1(b) and 1(d) have a very humble and modest representation of 'self'—really too small. Sample 1(d) looks like a question mark saying, 'Who am I?'. Sample 1(e) is tall and narrow rather like a plant drawn up to the light. Sample 1(f) has an initial loop attachment.

There is another very self-deprecating way of making an 'I' which is to use a small 'i'. The following two stories are about two very different types of people who used this 'i'. The first is from *Munby, Man of Two Worlds,* by Derek Hudson.

Austin Dobson, the poet, wrote an affectionate tribute to his friend Arthur Munby (Fig. 21), a Victorian barrister, poet, and civil servant. On Munby's death in 1910, Dobson said of his friend (who had 'pronounced opinions' on woman's rights and duties), that 'he has known many notables in art and letters and if his diaries should ever be published they could not fail to be interesting'.

What he did not know was that Munby left three deed boxes to his old college, Trinity, Cambridge, with the proviso that they were not to be opened until 1950. On January 14th of that year, the Master of Trinity G. M. Trevelyan duly opened the boxes. In them were notebooks, manuscripts, sketch books and a complete run of Munby's personal diaries from 1858 to 1898, which were of great value.

Munby, it appeared, had a fascination for working women of all kinds and had secretly married at Clerkenwell Parish Church an attractive Shropshire maidservant named Hannah Cullwick (Fig. 22). 'He had come to love her', said the will, 'with a pure and honourable love and not otherwise', but there had been one great snag; Hannah refused to become a 'lady'. She insisted on remaining Munby's servant, so he declared 'he had never been able to make known his marriage to his family'. Their life became very complex because of this; for example, his diaries say that when a clergyman friend called unexpectedly, '. . . making the best of the situation, I asked him to join me at dinner, and rang the bell. Instead of presenting our guest to my gentle graceful wife, and bidding him take the honour of a place by her at table, I had to treat her as one who served, and whom he would not care to notice.'

The deed box opened by the Master of Trinity College also contained a number of letters from Hannah; one dated September 14th, 1873, tells of her real personal joy in looking after her superior husband. Throughout the letter she used the small form of the letter 'i' instead of the capital one: '. . . i made my mind up that it was best and safest to be a slave to a gentleman, nor wife and equal to any vulgar man . . . i am as i am—a servant still, and a very low one . . . i am united in heart and soul as well as married at Church to the truest, best and handsomest man in my eyes that ever was born . . .'

The second story comes from Klara Roman's book, *Handwriting, a Key to Personality.* She writes about a young man who used this small form of the letter 'I' in his writing. He had run away from home at the age of thirteen and roamed about the country as a tramp. He worked as a handyman at a summer camp of artists. He was a talented but confused person, who regarded himself as worthless and useless; this self-devaluation was illustrated in his 'i'. One wonders whether someone noticing—perhaps a school teacher—when he began using this form of 'i', could not have built up his self-esteem and substantiated it before it was too late. The strength of writing is that the evidence is fixed and visible.

Returning to the chart, we see that the writer of sample 2(a) needs some emphasis in the U/Z of her ego symbol or, alternatively, some protection, in the guise of a hat. A hat provides a finishing touch and final emphasis to dress; it also gives protection from cold, wind, rain or hot sun. The writer of 2(b) needs emphasis in the M/Z in the form of a pedestal. A pedestal lifts you up from the level of ordinary folk. Writer 2(c) takes up space laterally. Writer 2(d) has turned his back on the past and is leaning forward, in a personal way, to face the future. Neither sample 2(e) nor 2(f) is a strong ego symbol—each faces in a different direction, one leaning in towards the future and one backing away from it. Sample 2(e) comes from the writing of a thirty-two year old unmarried lady, and 2(f) from a man who is a company director.

Samples 3(a), (b), (c) and (d) are all fractured 'I's; they have been made in two pieces. The best way to describe these people is to say that they have, for some reason or other, 'broken hearts' which have left them temporarily with no consolidated inner security. In 3(a) the split or fracture is much more marked and serious. In 3(e) there is damage of some sort in the ego. In sample 3(f) the 'I' looks as if it has a thorn sticking out of its head. This writer was suffering from schizophrenia.

The writers of samples 4(a) to (e) connect the capital 'I' to the next word. This is not a very rare occurrence over the general population. The 'I' can be connected with the word before or the word following. If it is connected to the word before, it could be that the inner personality is tied in some way to events in the past that cannot be shaken off. If the 'I' is connected to the following word, the writer needs someone to hold on to, or be with, in the present or foreseeable future. Samples 4(a) and (b) are both from writers whose 'ego' is attached to the past for some reason, and they cannot at the moment get away from it. The writers of 4(c) and (d) need someone to hold on to, and should not be left to live alone. Samples 4(e) and (f) are from the same writer, showing two different styles of the letter 'I', and therefore two aspects of self, in the same small example of writing.

Lines 5 and 6 show how the personal pronoun 'I' can be adapted and can appear in the shape of any number from 0–9. There are two aspects of the 'circle', 5(a). Firstly, the person inside is confined and enclosed; but secondly, the person inside is 'safe', with the circle providing a defence to the psyche from the dangers of 'without'. This form of 'I' was used consistently by a young

American girl who was in some turmoil due to the pressures of her current environment.

The only possible way to find out why someone does a thing is to ask, and in this way handwriting analysis can be detective work, provided the questioner is very careful and thoughtful as to how he poses the questions and when, so they do not invade personal privacy and become offensive. On asking about a writer who produced a perfect '2' as his 'I', the possible reason given by his mother was that he thought of himself as number '2'. His elder sister was always 'number 1'. When she went to school, his mother said, he insisted on laying another place at table for an imaginary person, so perhaps he was still number 2?

The writer of 7(a) may perhaps think of himself as a musical note. Sample 7(c) was written by a thirty-two year old man who has been married twice. His self-image is very involved and inflated; he is very 'tied up' in himself, and this likely causes difficulties for people sharing his world. He calls himself a mild schizoid personality. The writer of 7(d) is a girl of eighteen, an only child—perhaps she feels 'left out'? Sample 7(e) is from another only child, who wants to take up space laterally for himself; probably he never had to 'share space'. Sample 7(f) does not take up so much space laterally, but has a grasping movement in the M/Z. This movement appears to be in the process of developing in 7(e). Handwriting is frozen gesture and the gesture shown in this 'I' is one of the 'grasping hand'.

One more illustration of a slight variation on this form of 'I' shows how the same 'form' can be of greatly different significance in a different writing pattern:

Figure 23

> I am pleased to accept your offer, and the conditions attached thereto, and shall, therefore, report for work on Monday, May 10th, at 8.30 a.m.!*

This extract shows an example of the 'I' of Graham Young, the psychopath who was released from Broadmoor hospital for rehabilitation. He applied for, and got a job as an assistant storeman, and then proceeded to poison two of his fellow-workers, attempted to poison two more and administered poison to a further two before he was finally caught. An article in the *Observer* points out that poisoning as a crime is rare and male poisoners are more rare than female. Child male poisoners are rarer still, and child male poisoners who grow up to be adult male poisoners are limited to one—Graham Young. So it was not surprising that he confounded the experts. If we look at the way he makes his 'I', the start of the letter goes from right to left, whereas all copy-book forms of this style of 'I' proceed from left to right; this is a 'counter stroke', in the same way that the inverted 'I' was a counter stroke. So we can expect to find a 'social grasping' tendency, vested in a personality which is or wants to be unusual, non-conformist, different. This particular 'I' also has a break in the top. The rest of Graham Young's writing fills in the cold, clear-headed, purposeful personality in which this 'ego' lurks.

Sample 8(a) looks like a sword. The writer of 8(b) is a young girl from Thailand, writing in English. She came, unprotected and unworldly, into the hurly-burly of western student life and conceived herself, perhaps as being in an 'embryonic state'? Sample 8(c) is the 'I' of an elderly artist, showing tremor and using coloured ink. Aspects of 'colour' will be discussed in chapter 5. The writer of 8(d) is perhaps someone who thinks of himself as a 'sex symbol'—God's gift to women? Sample 8(e) appears to be from 'Mr Pound Note'. This 'I' has developed from Group 2 in the first chart. Sample 8(f) is a very interesting 'I'. In the 'I' of 8(e) the movement of the stroke went to the right in the U/Z and to the left in the M/Z and was the writing of a man. Sample 8(f) is the writing of a young woman of twenty-three years of age and the movements proceed to the left in the U/Z and to the right in the M/Z; the sample shows these two movements in 'balance', 'half and half', and is perhaps indicative of bisexuality.

The Archbishop of Canterbury, Dr Donald Coggan, said on television that the symbol of the Cross could be likened to the personal pronoun 'I' crossed through. He has illustrated what he meant. (See Fig. 24.) It is interesting that he does actually cross through his own 'I' when attaching it to the next word. One could interpret this as a 'denial of self in commitment to others'. In our examples, 4(c) and 4(d) are not crossed through, but 4(e) is. Sample 4(a) is also crossed through but this is a result of some attachment to the past.

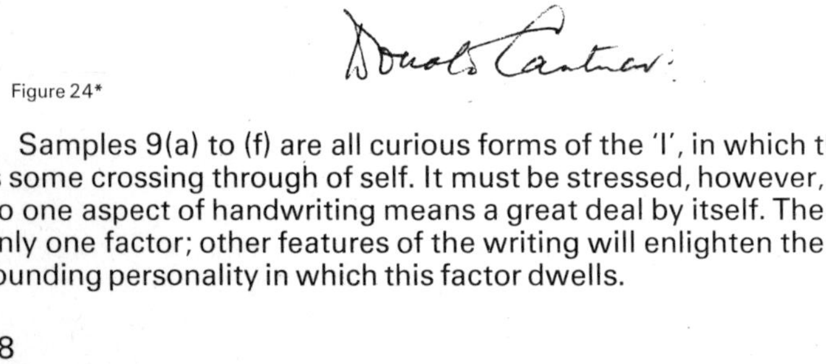

Figure 24*

Samples 9(a) to (f) are all curious forms of the 'I', in which there is some crossing through of self. It must be stressed, however, that no one aspect of handwriting means a great deal by itself. The 'I' is only one factor; other features of the writing will enlighten the surrounding personality in which this factor dwells.

Personal humility, the crossing through of self and the crossing out of strong ego manifestation, is central to Christianity. However, we also find in handwriting that the crossing out of the 'I' can in some cases be a sign of inner problems and self-destructive tendencies.

Signatures

Having looked at the symbolism of the personal pronoun 'I', the 'inner self', we must now move on to the symbolism of the signature, the 'public self'.

From early times, even in early pictographs, man has found it important to have some personal 'hallmark' for the outside world. His signature can be called his psychological identity card. It is entirely his own, manually produced and pictorially designed, both consciously and unconsciously, to suit his own aesthetic taste.

His signature represents his unique 'mark' as an entity in his family and also his endorsement, attestation and personal seal to confirm whatever he stands for or wishes to communicate to others and the outside world in general.

Young people early in life take pains to master the manual control needed to write their own names and get tremendous satisfaction from the achievement. Later on, their signature assumes more importance to them personally, and in adolescence, when they are literally 'finding themselves', they will often practise their signature on sheet after sheet of paper, endeavouring to evolve a design, embellishment, paraph or flourish which they think will suitably portray their image to other people. They may incorporate in their signature something of their father's signature, something of their Uncle Bob's, a bit from their favourite teacher or some pop star idol of the moment. All these are people they admire. They want to take essence from them, to absorb and make them a part of themselves. No one ever copies someone they dislike, despise or look down on.

Having evolved a signature, the design usually remains fairly constant throughout the individual's life, depending of course on what happens to him or her. He can grow tremendously in importance and his signature will grow with him in stature. He can have a breakdown or an accident which can be reflected in fractures, erosions and shrinkages which appear in the signature, as uncertainties and insecurities have developed in the personality itself.

A number of books give illustrations of the dramatic alterations in Napoleon's signature during his life. His signature as a young sub-lieutenant in 1791 is clear and legible, strong but not ostentatious. His later signature when at the height of his power is abbreviated but written with fierce strokes and pressure. Later, when he experiences disaster and defeat his signature becomes confused. When finally he is utterly defeated it dwindles to a shrivelled vanishing point.

Mr Charles Hamilton, a New York autograph dealer, and Mr Felix Lehmann, a handwriting analyst, produced these four examples of President Nixon's signature shown in Fig. 25.

Figure 25

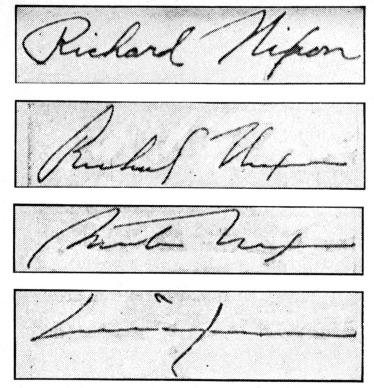

At the top of Fig. 25 is the signature of Richard Nixon in 1959. It appears to have plenty of vigour and drive, but notice how the exaggerated stroke of the 'x' is used to cross the name through. People often have premonitions of disaster and yet they are unable to quell or stifle the traits in their personality that drive them headlong towards it. In 1969 his signature shows severe shrinkage in the middle zone letters and the letter forms are blurred and illegible, showing that he is losing self-confidence and is uncertain of his image to the outside world. The third signature shows this process of shrinking becoming more marked, and the speed and drive more desperate. In the fourth signature the framework of the personality has gone; there is no strength, but more marked than ever is the crossing through of the void. The space taken up laterally remains fairly constant over the four signatures.

Placement of a signature is important and has the same implication with regard to left and right as we found in handwriting generally. If the signature is placed well over to the left, this can be a sign of withdrawal. A style of typing where the left margin is constant and the signature is in line to the left has been in vogue for some time, and was said to have originated in America. It is quicker and easier for the typist as the margin remains constant; perhaps it came in for this reason and was thought out by 'time and motion study' experts. However it is significant that it has been 'thought of' only in the last few years, as it may indicate a general withdrawal from the 'right' and thus a fear of the future.

In Lord Byron's signature the end stroke of the 'n' goes upwards and over the top of the word. This is a protective gesture, in the same way that a hand or hands can be put up to protect the head or face. Certainly Lord Byron's private life made him vulnerable and it is hardly surprising that he unconsciously made this shielding movement with his pen.

If this gesture is continued into a circle which surrounds the signature, the writer needs an enclosure to protect himself—this could be because of feelings of persecution, whether rooted in fact or in imagination.

Some signatures are very much smaller than the written text. The actual writing is the genuine attitude of the writer. The smaller signature is what he wants the outside world to think he is—that is, more modest and self-effacing than is in fact the case.

If the signature is much larger than the text, the reverse is true. Here is someone who gives claim to being a much 'larger' personality than he actually estimates himself.

If the Christian name of the signature is bold and legible but the surname dwindles or is illegible, the person may have unfortunate associations with their father or the family from whom the name comes; in the case of a married woman, it may indicate an unhappy relationship with her new name.

If you hold up a newly-received handwritten letter and notice that your name is written fairly small, and the signature is twice that size, you will know how the writer rates you compared to himself. If your name is very large and the writer's signature is very small, you will know that the writer is someone who holds you in high esteem.

Some signatures are totally illegible; what is more significant is the case of the busy high-powered executive who signs hundreds of letters and yet has a totally legible signature. He honours the document he signs because we know just exactly who he is. (Figs. 26 and 27.) Fig. 28 is the signature of Margaret Thatcher, the leader of the Conservative Party.

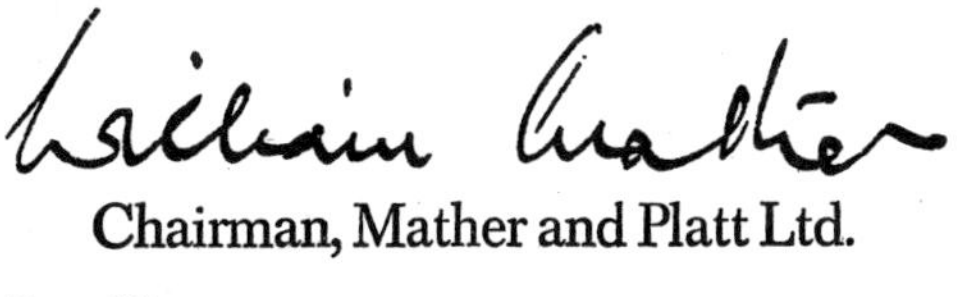

Chairman, Mather and Platt Ltd.

Figure 26*

Chairman, Thames Television Ltd.

Figure 27*

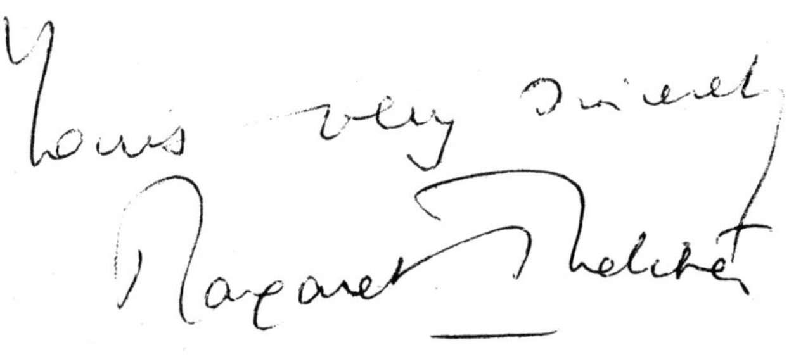

Figure 28

71

When signatures are totally divorced in style from the text of the writing, and look as if they are written by a different person, this can mean the signature is an outer disguise or mask to hide behind. The reason for the disguise can originate in fear, or in a need for self-protection; it can be a façade to hide an anti-social disposition.

Elaborate symbolism in signatures can evolve through the influence of a profession or an overriding interest; the writer himself may be unaware of this. Figs. 29 and 30 show the signatures of two pilots; one's signature is a design for a helicopter or whirly bird, the other underlines his very apt name with a paraph which is an exquisitely-drawn little jet plane.

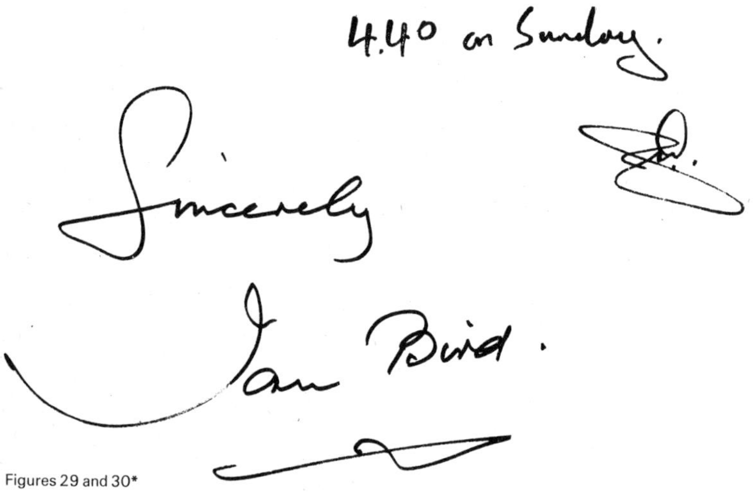

Figures 29 and 30*

Fig. 31 shows the signature of Lord Hunt, famous for leading his successful expedition up Mount Everest. Is the flag at the start of his signature the one they photographed at the top of Everest? And is the end 't' cross, going up, symbolic of a rope flung upwards for further heights to climb?

Figure 31

72

Writing is frozen gesture. In the signatures of these famous dancers we can see graceful movements, heads held high, glides, leaps, pirouettes and patterns.

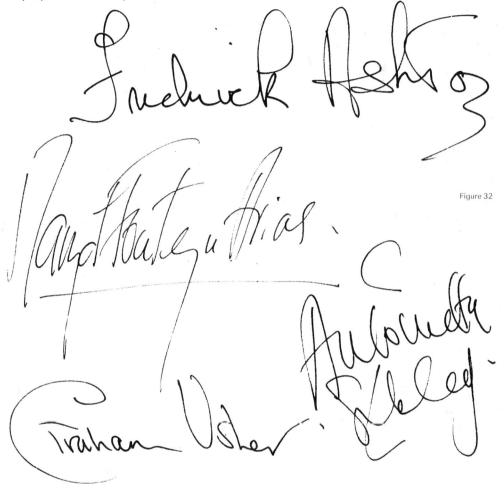

Figure 32

Another signature influenced by a profession? The writer of Fig. 33 is a Sales Director, selling cigarettes, perhaps a heavy smoker?

Figure 33

One more signature connected with smoke or steam, which we can see curling away, is that of James Watt (Fig. 34), inventor of the steam engine. Fig. 35 is the imaginative signature of an architect. Perhaps he designs high rise flats?

Figures 34 and 35

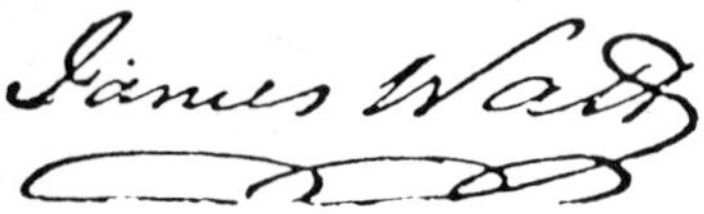

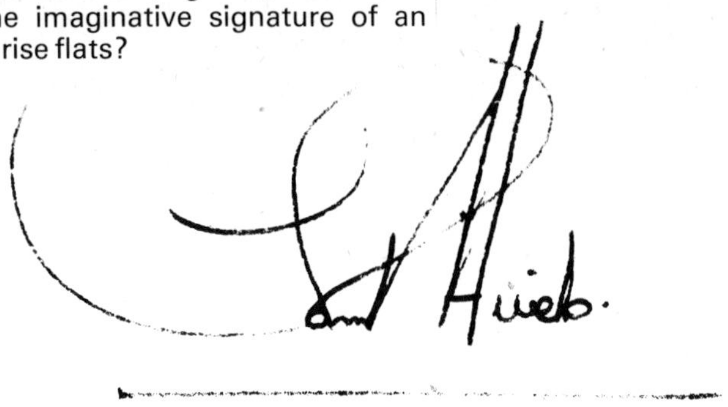

Fig. 36 shows another signature that must take infinite trouble to execute. Compare it with the signature from the Income Tax Inspector (Fig. 37). He is certainly a faceless civil servant.

Figure 36

Figure 37*

Fig. 38 is the signature of an official of the Henley rowing regatta. If you look at the signature from right to left, there is one stroke for the end of the boat, then eight oars, all rowing away. After this there are a few confused dots and dashes—staccatto instructions coming from the cox to his crew? Then there is the cox at the extreme left, with his controls!

Figure 38

Fig. 39 is the signature of the late Sir Gerald Nabarro. His moustache features symbolically in the design, from wing tip to wing tip!

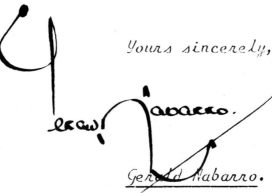

Yours sincerely,

Figure 39

74

Fig. 40 is an unusual cypher or hall mark. It is totally illegible and without further enlightenment we can only guess that the writer's public image is dominated or obsessed by something which involves the number three. As the three strokes intersect his writing, he may well feel threatened by them. Could it be golf three times a week—or fishing likewise? Unlikely! He may be involved with some technical process—these could be bobbins or lines. He is the only one who can unlock the symbolism, although he may not be conscious of it when he is writing.

Figure 40

Fig. 41 is another symbolic signature, but this time we know the answer—the signature bélongs to George Best. Outlined in the unconscious symbolism is the structure of his problem. The design content is that despite only two possible L/Z movements, in the two 'G's of George, he produces four. The capital 'B' in 'Best' is extended into the L/Z, as is the end of the 't'. Two goals? Four posts? They are all crossed through by the line emphasizing his own name and underlining his signature. The story of his life?

Figure 41

5 Special Features

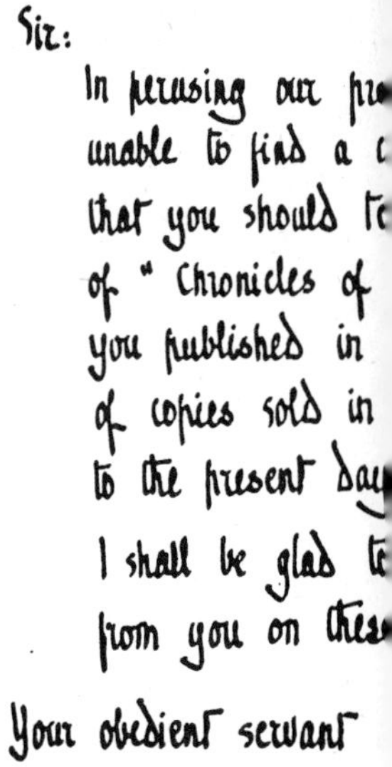

Legibility

Writing is a means of communication, so what are we to make of people who write and yet write illegibly? What is the point of the message if the receiver cannot understand it?

There would seem to be two reasons for illegible writing. Firstly the writer could not care less and is unconcerned as to whether you understand him or not. This type of illegible writer can be a brilliant research scientist, or someone who has become detached and lives in a world of his own thoughts. His thoughts may fly too fast for the hand to control them. He is unconcerned as to whether you can understand him or not.

Secondly, the writer actually may not want the person to know exactly what he has written for some reason or other. It is very easy if you do not know how to spell a word to write it somewhat illegibly to hide the possible wrong spelling. Doctors may often think that it is better for their patient's peace of mind not to know the exact nature of a prescription.

It is certainly inconsiderate to write illegibly; if your writing is illegible you may need to exert more self-discipline and care. Reginald Piggott, in his book, *Handwriting, A National Survey,* divided people into occupational groups for 'legibility of handwriting'. He found the top group for legibility was H.M. Services, all ranks, male and female. 18·3% wrote completely legibly, 40·1% were highly legible, 38·4% only moderately legible, 3·2% almost illegible. Next, with rather similar results came heavy manual workers of all grades, labourers, dockers, and miners. The most illegible writers were scientists and research workers, with 6·7% very legible, 30·1% fairly highly legible, 35·9% only moderately legible, and 23·4% almost illegible.

Doctors, medical students, chemists, dental surgeons, and nurses, were 9·1% completely legible, 51·2% fairly highly legible, 35·9% only moderately legible, 3·8% almost illegible. One answer to poor writing is to adopt a stylized type of writing. In Fig. 42 the writer tells us why he decided to change to 'Italic'.

People who change to Italic writing (Fig. 42) nearly always do it to cover some problem. They are frequently people who have been hurt by circumstances or events or they may be vulnerable through physical injury or disfigurement. They need to be insulated and protected from the real or imagined barbs of the world. Being landed

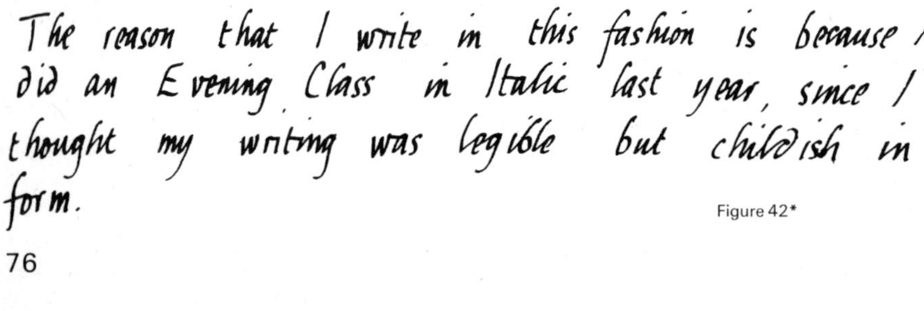

Sir:

In perusing our pr...
unable to find a c...
that you should r...
of "Chronicles of...
you published in...
of copies sold in...
to the present day...

I shall be glad to...
from you on these...

Your obedient servant

The reason that I write in this fashion is because I did an Evening Class in Italic last year, since I thought my writing was legible but childish in form.

Figure 42*

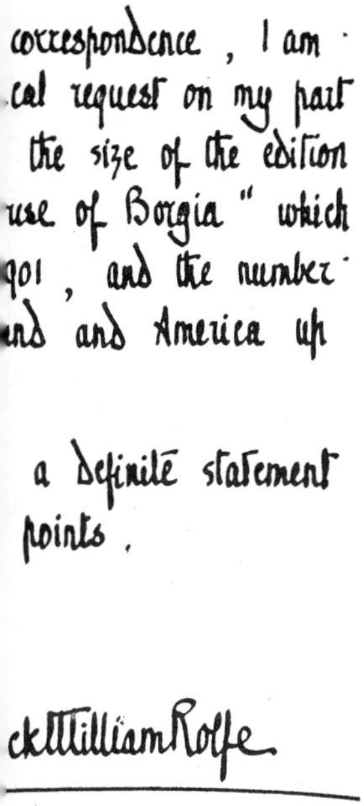

correspondence , I am ·
cal request on my part
the size of the edition
use of Borgia " which
901 , and the number·
and and America up

a definite statement
points .

cklWilliamRolfe

Figure 44*

with an unfortunate name can make difficulties and influence the personality development of a young person.

A very beautiful stylized writing is rather like a shop window shielding what is actually in the shop; it is 'putting on a good front'. This is a mask, and the personality is protected by it from the outside world. However, the mask also protects the outside from knowing what the problem is, and so from being able to understand and help. These people are Jung's 'persona' people. It is impossible to get past their screen or guard. They disappear and are insulated behind it. Dark glasses are another form of protection to hide behind, rather like 'blinds' for windows; the people inside can see out but those outside cannot see in.

Fig. 43 shows another type of stylized writing. People who have a natural spontaneous writing of their own should not be confused with calligraphers or sign writers who study the craft and art of beautiful writing for manuscripts, sign boards, decoration, or advertisements.

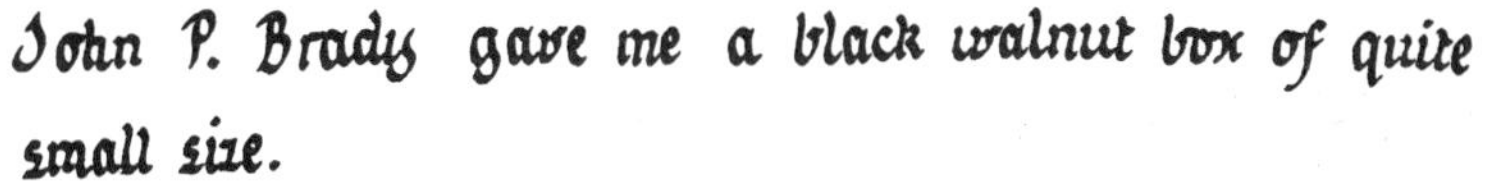

John P. Brady gave me a black walnut box of quite small size.

Figure 43*

Fig. 44 is the writing of that eccentric genius Frederick William Rolfe, author of many books and verses, some under the assumed name of Baron Corvo, the best known being *Hadrian the Seventh.* His handwriting is aesthetically a disciplined and stylised work of art. A polished, carefully cultivated protection and façade for the intense, frightened person inside.

Left-handedness

The Greek philosopher Anaxagoras, who lived about 500 B.C. is said to have maintained that man owed all his wisdom, knowledge, and superiority over animals to the use of his hands.

The tools used by early man give evidence that he was ambidextrous. Paul Sarasin examined a number of primitive weapons and found that 135 were intended for lefthanders, 146 for right hands and 145 for both hands. It is interesting that babies show no hand preference.

There are numerous theories for the dominance of the right hand. Thomas Carlyle's 'primitive warfare' theory held that man became right-handed so that the left hand could hold the shield and thus protect the heart. On this basis left-handers were much more vulnerable and less likely to survive with hearts unprotected in hand-to-hand fighting.

Other theories on handedness have a medical basis, one being called the 'mechanical theory', which gives the right side an advantage because of the displacement of the centre of gravity in the body. According to this theory, the greater weight of the liver and lungs on the right enables a man to balance better on the left foot, leaving the right hand free for action.

'Natural selection' or 'instinct' could influence handedness. A disposition to handedness could be inherited, and therefore have an organic base. It could be decided by the blood supply to the brain, or the superior development of one cerebral hemisphere, or by ocular dominance. There are numerous possibilities.

The nature/nurture argument which pervades theories of personality development is just as evident in handedness. It could be influenced by habit, upbringing, or early education. Each discipline and investigator can evolve a theory that fits in best with his chosen speciality and with what he is setting out to prove.

Left-handedness can have an hereditary base or it can be influenced by early training. Hand dominance is a form of adaptation by the individual to the environment. Left-handedness can be an additional or coincidental effect of an underlying emotional or learning disturbance. We have seen that in handwriting, there is a connection between 'left slant' and negative attitudes. So left-handedness can stem from veering from what is right or what is expected of one.

The fact is that we live in a right-handed world and the left-hander starting out in life is swimming against the prevailing stream; although the current of the stream is not powerful, it is there. His path through life will not be eased by using the left hand. Stuttering and allied difficulties have been found to result from forcing the left-hander to use the right, but numerous people make the change and achieve right-handed writing with no ill effects.

In Fig. 45 the writer tells us how he changed to his right hand for writing; his writing is clear, legible, balanced and flows rhythmically along. It seems that the way the training is done is im-

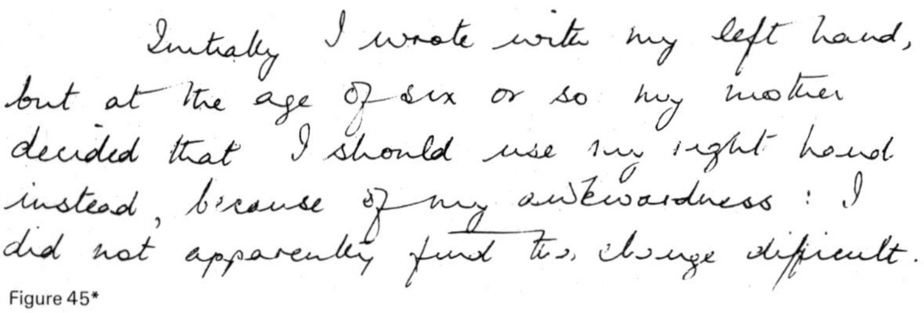

Initially I wrote with my left hand, but at the age of six or so my mother decided that I should use my right hand instead, because of my awkwardness: I did not apparently find the change difficult.

Figure 45*

portant; if it can be done early, tactfully, persuasively and with encouragement and praise, the child will benefit from conforming. However, aggressive forcing against a real determination for the left can leave a residue of damage.

In 1860, 2% of the population were left-handed. Today the national average in Britain is about 8% and probably higher, with more men than women being left-handed. The manual difficulty of writing is very much greater for left-handers. However, in the Mensa survey (Fig. 46), 32% of the left-handed participants chose

Slant—Percentages					
	Left slant (marked)	Left slant (slight)	Upright	Right slant (slight)	Right slant (marked)
All writings in the survey	4	10	34	34	18
Males	4	10	32	33	21
Females	6	11	39	33	11
Married	3	8	32	32	24
Single	5	13	36	34	12
Single and over the average age of marriage	1	11	33	38	17
Grammar school	6	10	31	36	17
Public school	3	12	40	28	17
Left-handers	5	20	47	27	5
Right-handers	4	10	33	34	19
Only children— male	5	15	35	30	15
Only children— female	8	11	41	30	10
Only children all	6	14	36	30	14

Figure 46

a right slant, while only 25% chose a left one.

A substantial increase in left-handedness has come with the 'permissive society'. Reginald Piggott in his *Handwriting, A National Survey,* found out how many left-handers there were in different professional groups. In clergy of all denominations there were 1·9%, artists, painters, sculptors, 8·8%, and students, 13·2%. This was by far the highest group and it is probably higher still today.

The word 'sinister' is the Latin for 'left'. It also means unlucky, perverse, or bad. In English 'sinister' means ominous, mysteriously wicked, or evil. 'Right' comes from the Latin 'rectus', which means straight, erect, or just. In traditional pantomimes, the good fairy enters from the right of the stage while the wicked magician makes his entrance from the left. Are the ominous implications of the 'left' all a legacy from early taboos?

Some experts say they can easily tell if a writer is left-handed just by looking at his script. Test yourself on the eight writings in Fig. 47. The answers are given in the Appendix at the back of the book.

Figure 47*

1. It is now fair to state that quite possibly, the nature of our relationship with the universe is that of any living thing within the confines of another living thing.

2. We regret that lack of space has prevented us from publishing all the letters we have received.

3. The more time I have the less I do, but the more time I do, the less I have.

4. When in Rome do as the Romans do.

5. Because this is written in the train, my handwriting may be somewhat more shaky than usual.

6. How should I tell my fiancé that I no longer love her?

7. 'Whatever his weight in pounds shillings + ounces he always seems bigger because of his bounces.'

8. A fascinating expertise is that of the graphologist. Merely to think of him (or her) makes me slow down and become less obviously depraved and slovenly.

Colour

One other subject which has an association with writing is individual colour preference, in choice of paper and ink. In a recent survey of 2,000 writings, 62% chose to write with blue ink or blue ball-point pens, 36% with black and 2% with other colours—red, green, and violet. There could, of course, be an element of chance in this—borrowing a pen or picking up one that happened to be available. However, the selection of these last colours is comparatively rare in writing.

It is interesting to ponder colour preference. Personal likes and dislikes regarding colour can be definite at the time of selection and can depend on the state of mind and the glandular balance of the person. What you like at one time you may not like a year or so later. The colours that suit you change as you grow older. We can go into a friend's house and wonder how could they possibly live with the colours they have chosen.

Colour vision appears to be related both to the educated and to the primitive part of the brain, so man's early experience of 'colour' can motivate us instinctively. To very early man, who got up at sunrise and settled down to sleep at sunset, dark blue meant evening, the coming of night, and with it a time to end the hard work and activity of the day, a time to be peaceful, calm, quiet, to rest and sleep. Blue was also connected with the heights and infinity of the sky and with the depths and tranquility of the sea.

On the other hand the 'yellow' of the early dawn, the wonder of the rising sun, gave rise to activity, hope for new achievements, the excitement of chance and development in the day ahead. In spring, the start of the year, many of the flowers are yellow.

When man was out hunting, his blood was pulsing with emotion; he was pitting his wits against danger for his very survival. The hunt could result in blood spilt, either his own or that of his quarry. Therefore red was associated with emotion, danger, fire, the vital living force of blood. Primitive man would stain with red anything he wanted to bring to life.

Green was the colour of vegetation, growing things which persisted and provided nourishment; they represented self-preservation and were tangible and passive, a part of every day existence.

White implied innocence, the beginning, the empty page on which the story was to be written. It also stood for the clean purity of snow, the wisdom of old age, the shining light of the gods, the supernatural. Sacred horses were white.

Brown was the colour of the earth. Black, a non colour, and the opposite of white, was connected with mystery, the frightening time of dead of night, sleep and dreams, the unconscious, the unknown; in some cultures, it meant death, putting out the light, the ending.

Red, orange and yellow are warm colours associated with 'release'. Blue, indigo and violet are cold colours associated with the opposite tendency, 'tension'. You can be blue with cold or have 'the blues', which is a depressing experience.

If you stare at 'red' and fix your attention on it you will find your heart beat and breathing speed up. Red is exciting and emotional. The red light of the brothel is emotive. We talk of a 'red rag to a bull', we can 'see red'; red is also for 'danger'. The school master can lacerate one's carefully executed homework with red ink.

Dark blue gives a sense of harmony and quiet, and is the most suitable colour for meditation. If you stare at blue it has a calming effect; blue is associated with sweetness, devotion, thinking and religious feeling.

Going out for an evening meal and erotic entertainment, a mysterious decor of red, orange, gold and black heightens the emotions, enlivens and enhances pleasurable excitement. Would it give a feeling of tranquillity and ease to set out in an aeroplane, so decorated, for a flight over the pole?

Yellow indicates the far-seeing sun, a coming from darkness into light, and thus the faculty of intuition. Yellow was the colour of the Chinese royal family and of deities and royalty who were associated with the sun.

Green is a bridge between blue and yellow, a defensive passive colour. It can mean inexperience or unripeness, and can have an astringent suggestion. You can be 'green with envy'. Sugar will never sell wrapped up in green packets; it must be associated with blue for sweetness.

Violet is a mixture of blue and red; a choice of violet can indicate emotional insecurity or glandular imbalance. It is also connected with mystery, nostalgia and memories.

Grey is a dreary colour. It stands for neither dark nor light, neither tension nor release; it is symptomatic of indifference and non-involvement, in the same way that upright writing is neutral, neither 'for' nor 'against'. Sombre grey skies over a number of days can be depressing. One can also be 'black' with despair.

The symbolism of pictorial imagery, space and colour, is universal, and applies to people old and young, educated or uneducated, the world over. The paintings of young children can be a pictorial weathervane of their innermost feelings. In painting a picture of his family, a child will portray in colours and spatial arrangement his own impression of how he fits into the family circle and his own relationships within it.

We have seen some of the implications of colour; it is not difficult to see how a child feels if he paints himself dark—in greys and blacks—with everyone else in bright colours. Mother, who is warm, life-giving, and loving, is often painted in red. However, a parent with a very red face can be 'scarlet with anger'. The child may then picture himself as very small in size and on the left of this forbidding figure. Father, the senior member of the family, the person who came first, the bread-winner and head of the family, is often coloured blue, the colour of the sky that we look up to. Many fathers that leave for work early and come home late, or are often away on business, are 'unknown' rather mysterious figures in the eyes of their children, and can therefore be painted in black or grey.

Father is usually placed on the left of the family group, then mother, then all the children in order of seniority. Left-handers will often reverse this order and have father on the extreme right. If there is no father in the family, mother will very often be in the centre of the group with the children on either side. A sad, rejected child may demur or decline if asked to paint the family, or he may paint himself away from the group, smaller than everyone else. He may leave his image of himself unfinished, sightless, or without hands and feet, or he may totally exclude himself from the group, not feeling a part of it.

Fig. 48 (p. 63) shows 'my family' painted by Paul, aged seven years. He is the one in violet. Father is there in blue smoking his pipe, then mother in a red hat, an older brother in green, and a much-loved younger brother in red. On a different plane to the family is their dog. Above stands their house. The house is depicted in black but the door and interior of the house appear gay and bright. We find on inquiring that Paul has only just moved to this new house, which is still strange and 'unknown' to him. A bright yellow sun shines down on this family.

Through the medium of colour we can look into the child's world without asking questions, and we can use the information so gained to understand and to help him.

Young people and handwriting

If a personality assessment is to be made from writing, the writer must have reached the degree of writing fluency discussed in Chapter 2, where the mind is occupied with ideas and sentences and not at all with the manual manipulations of writing.

A child is still occupied with the technical feat of mastering letter forms. Children's writing is not suitable for analysis in the way that adult writing is. However, the basic principles of handwriting analysis apply to every writing. A child's progress can be followed by his handwriting achievement. If an example of current writing is taken every few months, the development of the writing will mirror the child's advances, as well as any setbacks through physical illness or injury. This will be a time of continual experimentation and change.

Some children are adventurous, unpredictable and non-conformist; others are cautious, placid and try immensely hard to conform and please. In some schools a rigid handwriting programme and strong discipline are the order of the day. Very often the Italic script is taught; this is good for discipline and technical control. The conformist type of child will thrive on this and be praised for his ability to reproduce this rigid style of writing. The teacher similarly will be delighted to exhibit the uniform technical skills of her pupils. Fig. 49 shows the italic writing of two ten year old twins. The non-conformist type of pupil will find this style of writing frustrating and very difficult to master; he will continually have trouble with the symmetry of his letters.

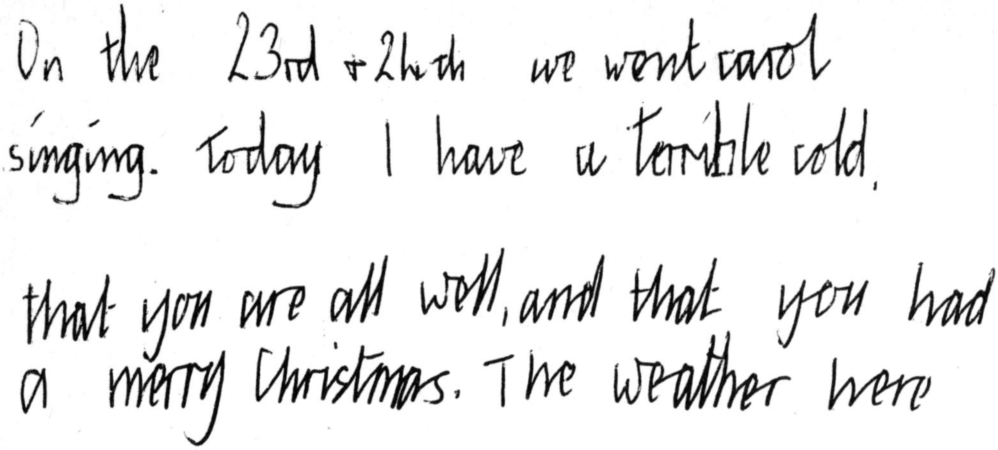

On the 23rd & 24th we went carol singing. Today I have a terrible cold, that you are all well, and that you had a merry Christmas. The weather here

Figure 49

In another type of school where the emphasis is on 'free expression' the development of individual styles from letter forms is encouraged. The adventurous type of child will flourish but the more cautious one will find himself a bit at sea, preferring and feeling more secure in a disciplined, structured situation. The best of both worlds is ideal, with the child being able to develop his own natural, comfortable, easily legible writing within a steady framework.

Ruth Mock, an art teacher, and V. E. C. Gordon, a school inspector, wrote a book called *20th Century Handwriting*. Fig. 50 shows their recommended specimen alphabet and copy-book form, which any handwriting analyst would endorse, apart from altering the formation of the 'b' in their cursive alphabet to ' *b* '.

ABCDEFGHIJKLMNOPQRSTUVWXYZ

abcdefghijklmnopqrstuvwxyz

Print script alphabet for the infant school

ABCDEFGHIJKLMNOPQRSTUVWXYZ

abcdefghijklmnopqrstuvwxyz

abcdefghijklmnopqrstuvwxyz

Figure 50

A sound working knowledge of handwriting analysis can be invaluable to a writing teacher. She can 'tone down' the self-display of the very large writer, while encouraging and boosting the ego of the very small writer. The writers of very narrow, squeezed letter forms will be afraid to talk; they need to be given confidence and helped to 'open up'. Encouraging expansive movements physically, wide steps and gestures, as well as wider written letters, can help the very inhibited child, and help is badly needed at this stage, if we are to avoid producing so many painfully inhibited adults. They turn up at interviews for jobs and cannot do justice to themselves or put themselves 'over', because they are so cramped, restricted and bottled up inside.

Young people that make very large spaces between their words are often lonely and isolated; they need help and understanding to draw them into a close group of friends. Sudden alterations in the writing of young people can be a warning that all is not well. Continual alteration and 'mending' of letters is a sign of mental irritation. Writing sinking down below the line can be caused by physical ill health, depression, or general fatigue. The child may not be getting enough sleep.

At the onset of puberty an adolescent's writing, which may previously have been neat and disciplined, may change—the slant may go in all directions or noticeably more to the left. This is an unsettling time; a young person feels vulnerable and is trying to find his true role and identity as an adult. Many young people adopt a left slant at this time as a defensive gesture. This can indicate a reluctance to leave childhood and the past behind and a fear of plunging into the unknown adult world. At this time developing sexuality may alarm boys and girls and can be shown in crippled underlengths which turn to the left. Fig. 51 shows changes in a boy's writing: (a) was written when he was thirteen years old, and (b) when he was sixteen.

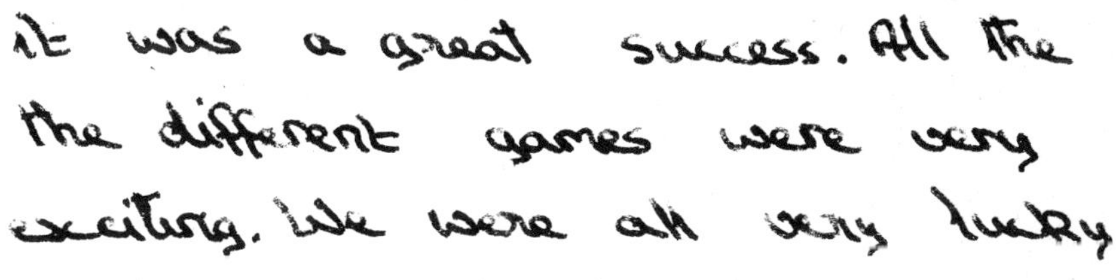

Figure 51(a)

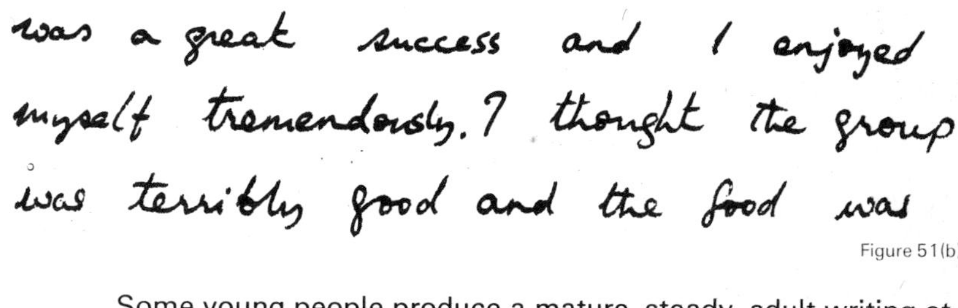

Figure 51(b)

Some young people produce a mature, steady, adult writing at fourteen years old or earlier but others are still in an unsettled state and may not produce an adult style of writing until well in their twenties, if at all. The mobility of families at the present time means that some children are continually changing schools. If they have developed a natural legible writing it seems sad that on arriving at a new school they are often forced to change to the style of writing preferred at that school. Over a number of changes this can have a stultifying effect.

Marty Stewart, a handwriting analyst who has made a special study of children's writing, says, 'If a normally bright and happy child is using the available space on the paper in a bizarre way which indicates that he has little or no idea of 'top', 'bottom', 'right' or 'left', he may well have a perceptual difficulty which should be investigated and helped early.' It is of little use to try to teach children to read and write before they have mastered the basic skills of relating to space, judging distance, the control of hand movements, the remembering of simple sounds, the remembering of simple shapes, and the co-ordination between all these and the eyes.

This co-ordination, instantaneous and accurate, is needed to achieve meaningful symbols and join them into words on a page, as in writing. Accurate recall of shape and sound and meaning, as in reading, cannot be achieved without them. If there is a serious 'lag' in the development of any or all of these functions, unusual difficulties and, at times, complete blocks can occur.

A lack of correct spatial perception results from a condition known as dyslexia. It has nothing to do with intelligence; it happens to very slow as well as very bright children, and more often to boys than girls. It can be an inherited tendency; three out of five brothers can have it. These children have to work incredibly hard to achieve modest writing, reading and spelling skills. Help by experienced teachers must be given to them as early as possible; first, to develop their lagging perceptual functions and their co-ordination, and second, to nurture their often outstanding compensatory abilities. Confidence in themselves as able people is more important to these children than reading and writing. Their lives will be difficult in our society but they can learn how to cope with this problem. If a child, otherwise bright and happy, begins to wilt at school and produces unusually slow, clumsy, uncertain, disorganized letter-forms, written with unusually hard, anxious pressure, often with reversals, upside-down letters, and amendments, with mirror-writing persisting after the age of eight years, and letters refusing to sit on the line, an investigation is most certainly advisable.

6 How Handwriting Analysis Can Help

Vocational Guidance

One of the most important decisions a person makes in his or her life is the choice of a career. Young people setting out on a career may get help from their parents, their careers master at school, and their local careers officer—each has a special knowledge or skill to contribute.

In addition to these, the analysis of handwriting can provide an extra source of help and encouragement by giving an objective evaluation of personality strengths and weaknesses. John L. Holland in his book *The Psychology of Vocational Choice* describes six personality types which are recognizable from handwriting. It is only possible in this small book to give a rough outline of these types, one writing example and some preferred occupations.

(1) The Realistic Type

Actively participates with tools and machines to do a concrete task, avoids intellectualism, is hard and aggressive, not a socially sensitive person.
Writing example Chapter 2, 6(c) page 27; an angular style of writing in which all letters are connected.
Occupations engineer, electrician, plumber, tree surgeon, aircraft mechanic

(2) The Intellectual Type

Prefers to think through rather than act out problems, tends to be unconventional and likes ambiguous tasks.
Writing example Chapter 2, 8(c) page 28; small writing with very clear spacing and clever letter connections.
Occupations zoologist, geologist, physicist, writer of scientific articles

(3) The Social Type

Works through emotions and feelings, is good with people, needs social interaction, is concerned and wants to help and influence the poor, the sick and the unfortunate.
Writing example Chapter 2, 7(d) page 28; rounded broad writing with garland connections.
Occupations speech therapist, world peace organiser, case worker, missionary, nurse, school teacher

(4) The Conventional Type

A conforming person, does not like ambiguous work situations, is good at routine and well structured tasks, values status.
Writing example Chapter 2, 7(c) page 27; regular, connected writing with copybook connections.
Occupations statistician, bank clerk, book keeper, local government officer, civil servant

(5) The Enterprising Type

Adventurous, enthusiastic, good at selling, persuading, influencing, dominating; prefers ambiguous ill-defined situations, does not like monotonous, confining work.

Writing example Chapter 2, 5(c) page 26; right slant, broad, fairly large writing with fluid letter forms.

Occupations salesman, sports promoter, agent, politician, business executive

(6) The Artistic Type

Needs individual expression, likes to work through self-expression, usually not sociable, avoids problems that are highly structured.

Writing example Chapter 2, 4(c) page 25; controlled stylised writing, with original letter forms and aesthetically beautiful spacing; or unusual, dynamic, irregular writing, sometimes with hectic disarray.

Occupations artist, designer, freelance writer, stage director, musician

Some people belong to only one 'type', but others have a vocational role which can cover two or three 'types'. For instance, an engineer can be employed on construction on a concrete task (1), or on intellectual research in the engineering field (1 and 2). He can teach engineering (1 and 3), or he can be employed by the council as borough engineer (1 and 4). He can sell and promote engineering products (1 and 5) or he can be employed on the design side in engineering (1 and 6). If he was an engineer on the selling, promoting and advertising side he very likely would combine 1, 5, and 6. There are numerous applications in any given field.

Personnel selection

Graphology can be very useful as an additional aid in personnel selection both for the employer and for the employee. It is just as important for the new graduate or school leaver seeking employment for the first time to get into the right job as it is for the employer to select and train the right person for his firm. A clear picture of the use of graphology in personnel selection is given in the book *Handwriting Analysis in Business*. (See *Further Reading*.)

In a large company, which has its own personnel department, graphology can be used as a source of additional information on candidates short-listed for top level jobs. In a medium-sized concern, where the directors have to do their own staff selection, graphology can be very helpful if used in addition to the usual tests, group discussions and personal interviews. Graphology covers aspects of personality not covered in other tests. In a small business where the boss picks his own staff on the basis of a personal interview alone, graphology can be extremely useful to confirm views, and give a second opinion in the event of any doubts. It can also give pointers as to further inquiries to be made. If you are thinking of going into partnership with a colleague or some unknown business associate, an assessment of compatibility from writing would be a very sound step to take.

The following personal details of the writer are required for a graphologist to make a report: (a) age of applicant, (b) sex of applicant, (c) nationality of applicant or, if possible, country in which he learned to write.

The best possible material to work from is a recent letter written spontaneously and without any thought that the handwriting might be analysed, plus notes not written specially. A signature is also important. Obviously the more writing the graphologist has to work from the more detailed the report he can produce. It is also important for the graphologist to have a brief job analysis of the appointment being considered, and a list of any working qualities which are especially important in this job.

As there is no recognized professional qualification for graphologists, the graphologist should provide a reference on the standard of his work from another firm, or failing that, he could be given a test using the writing of one or two employees who have failed in the job as well as one or two who were successful.

Police work

A graphologist can be called a 'handwriting consultant', but the designation of 'handwriting expert' usually refers to an expert witness called to give evidence in court, as to the similarity or disparity of a questioned example of handwriting.

Mr D. M. Ellen, the Principal Scientific Officer of the Metropolitan Police Forensic Science Laboratory, Documents Division, is reluctant to call himself a 'handwriting expert', preferring the title of 'document examiner'.

The police have forensic science laboratories for the scientific examination of questioned blood samples, finger prints, etc., and a similar laboratory for the scientific examination of questioned documents. The people employed in the laboratory as document examiners are all science graduates, at the moment mostly chemists; new science graduates making a career in document examination have a year on probation, learning how to study writing and how to prepare their evidence for presentation in court.

For the document examiner, an objective scientific approach to the subject is imperative; to quote Wilson R. Harrison, 'No opinions except those based on evidence, and what cannot be demonstrated is not evidence.' However, Mr Ellen admits that one of the chief difficulties the scientific document examiner has to face is the lack of 'groups' and 'types' for writing which they have for blood and finger prints, and the lack of 'tables of probability'. He says they try hard to keep a balance between fairness and caution, and often findings have to be couched in phrases such as 'there is a high probability', 'this could have come from', 'we cannot exclude the possibility that', or 'no evidence that'. The more you know about handwriting, the more you are aware of how much there is still to learn.

Masculine and feminine traits in handwriting

No graphologist or handwriting expert can tell the age or sex of a writer. The reason for this is that the phenomena that shape and inspire writing stem from psychic, mental force, not physical force. As mentioned in Chapter 3 we can think of it as 'brain' writing, not 'hand' writing. On a mental level we can have so-called 'masculine' women and 'feminine' men. There is a feminine/masculine spectrum that covers the whole field.

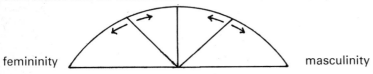

femininity   masculinity

If you are a man with a mental outlook on the feminine side of the scale your writing will show 'feminine' characteristics, and vice versa if you are a female with a 'masculine outlook'. Numerous people say they can always tell the sex of a writer. If you are one of them, test yourself on the following examples (Fig. 52). Fifty per cent success is average! The answers are given in the Appendix at the back of the book.

Figure 52*

1   No spring, nor summer beauty hath such grace as I have seen in one autumnal face.

2   Force is the mid-wife at the birth of a new social order.

3   There are two ways to get to the top of an oak tree – you can climb it or you can sit on an acorn.

4   In the general calamities of mankind, the death of an individual, however exalted, the ruin of an edifice, however famous, are passed over with careless inattention

5 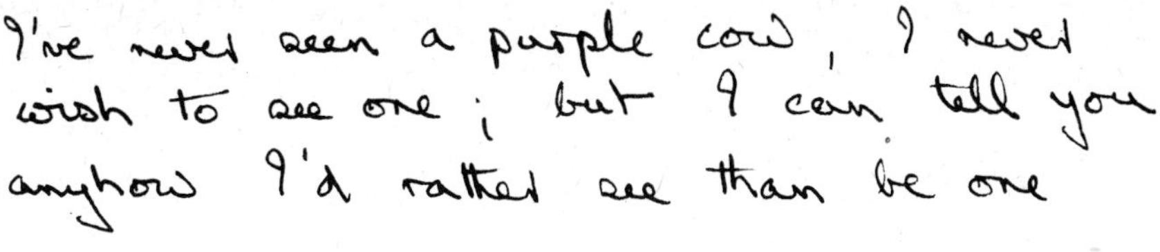 I've never seen a purple cow, I never wish to see one; but I can tell you anyhow I'd rather see than be one

6 Habit, I was deaf, dumb, blind, and paralytic to a million things, from habit.

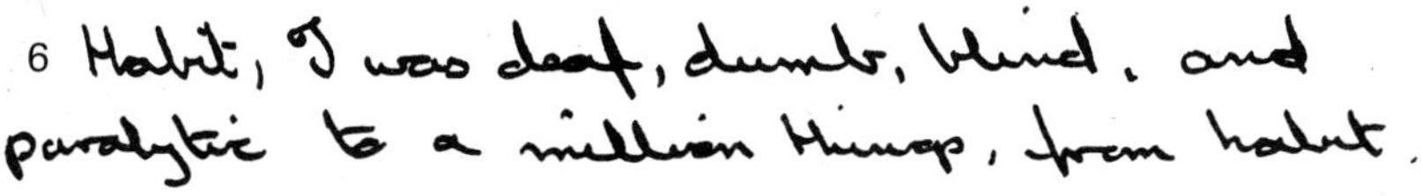

Since we are dealing with expressions of 'mind', physical age leaves no mark on it. Very young people can be extremely mature and competent. Other people can journey through life with un-settled, immature personalities that never 'set' and mature. Old people frequently can be very childish. If you think you can easily tell the age of a writer, test yourself on the samples in Fig. 53. The answers are given in the Appendix.

1 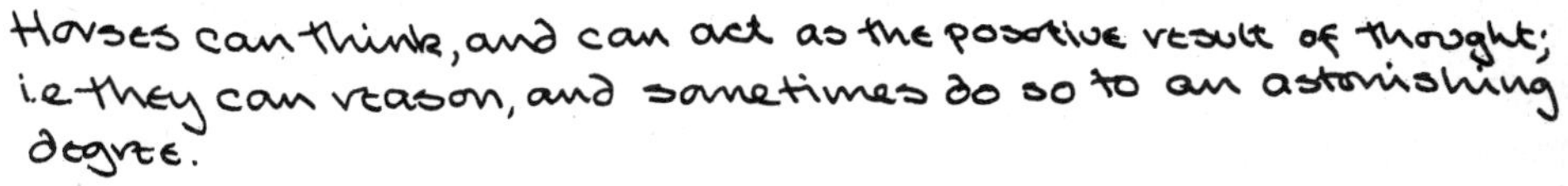 Horses can think, and can act as the positive result of thought; i.e. they can reason, and sometimes do so to an astonishing degree.

2  This offers a temptation to which I will not yield!

3 Retma had already pronounced the epitaph for Man: "We did not have time to find out all we wanted to know."

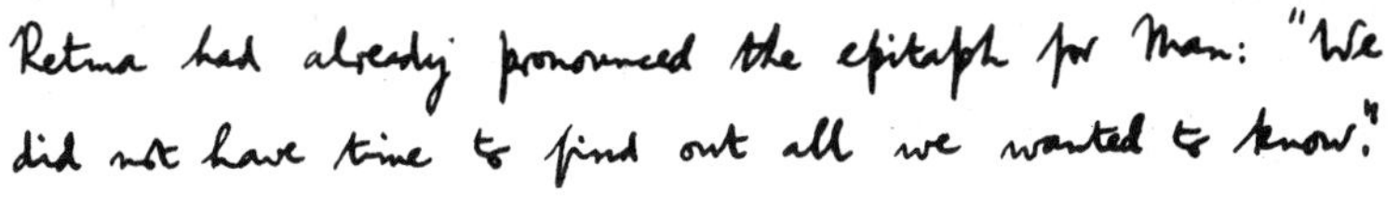

4 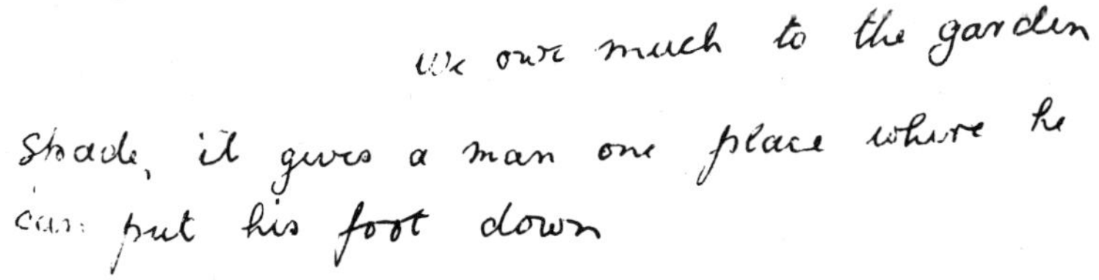 We owe much to the garden shade, it gives a man one place where he can put his foot down

5  It is very showery today.

6 Some men are wise, and some are otherwise.

Figure 53*

Applied graphology is an art. The way it is applied rests in the hands of the individual. Sir Bernard Lovell, in a biographical programme on television said, 'As a man sees so he is.' Each person sees with his own eyes, his own experience of life, his own position in society, his own prejudices and tastes. No two people have the same set of memories and experiences to influence the picture they see.

Different people in possession of the same set of facts, when asked to transpose them into words, will produce different reports, each of which has an individual personal stamp, in wording, arrangement and presentation.

Students who study a specific course within a defined curriculum and a carefully devised learning scheme, end up with a universal approach and standard building bricks of knowledge which have been placed in their minds to build their particular house. Everyone on the course goes through the steps and can finally construct a similar house.

There is no recognized training for graphologists in Britain. This is not a subject that you can teach yourself; it must be learned on a course or from an expert. If everyone learns individually and approaches the subject from different directions, there will be a disparity in the standard of work they achieve; they will all produce unique houses, none of them built to a recognized design.

The layman has no way of knowing what grasp or depth of knowledge a so-called expert may have. He may just have read a few books on the subject and then trusted to intuition and native sharpness to bluff his way along.

Established disciplines do not suffer from 'pop' aspects of their subject, because they have solid foundations of learning. The foundations of graphology in Britain have not yet been soundly laid. This is an intimate subject that has a tremendous potential to help in the field of personality study, if it is given the chance.

If through reading this book you have gained a better understanding of yourself r. those whom you love —

perhaps a ripple may
go out from this to a
better understanding in
the world at large —
It is a vain hope but
I leave you with it

Jane Paterson

APPENDIX

Answers to quiz on handedness

(1) 23 male single
bookseller
left-handed

(2) 20 female married
secretary
right-handed

(3) 21 male single
salesman
right-handed

(4) 15 female single
school girl
left-handed

(5) 53 male married
civil servant
left-handed

(6) 22 male single
accounts clerk
left-handed

(7) 29 female single
lecturer
right-handed

(8) 49 male married
RAF officer
naturally left-handed,
forced to use right hand

Answers to quiz on the sex of the writer

(1) 25 female single
teacher

(2) 54 male married
self-employed businessman

(3) 16 male single
student

(4) 55 female married
teacher

(5) 38 male single
chartered accountant

(6) 22 female single
teacher

Answers to quiz on age

(1) 14 female single
school girl

(2) 51 male married
doctor

(3) 25 male single
civil servant

(4) 67 female married
housewife

(5) 50 female married
housewife

(6) 19 female single
student

FURTHER READING

Currer-Briggs, Noel, Kennet, Brian, and Paterson, Jane *Handwriting Analysis in Business*
   Associated Business Programmes
Gordon, V. E. C. and Mock, Ruth *Twentieth Century Handwriting* Methuen
Gray, William S. *The Teaching of Reading and Writing* UNESCO and Scott, Foresman
   & Co.
Green, Janet Nugent *You and Your Private Eye* Llewellyn Publications, St Paul,
   Minnesota
Hamilton, Charles *Collecting Autographs and Manuscripts* University of Oklahoma
Hartford, Hunting *You Are What You Write* Macmillan Inc, New York
Hearns, Rudolph *Handwriting and Analysis through its Symbolism* Vantage Press, Inc
Jacoby, H. J. *Analysis of Handwriting* George Allen & Unwin
Mendel, Alfred *Personality in Handwriting* Peter Owen
Meyer, Oscar N. *The Language of Handwriting* Peter Owen
Munby, A. N. L. *The Cult of the Autograph Letter in England* Athlone Press
Olyanova, Nadya *The Psychology of Handwriting* Sterling, New York
Piggott, Reginald *Handwriting – A National Survey* George Allen & Unwin
Rawlins, Ray *Four Hundred Years of British Autographs* J. M. Dent
Rice, Louise *Character Reading from Handwriting* Frederick A. Stokes, New York
Roman, Klara *Handwriting – A Key to Personality* Routledge & Kegan Paul
Saudek, Robert *Experiments with Handwriting* George Allen & Unwin
   The Psychology of Handwriting George Allen & Unwin
Singer, Eric *Personality and Handwriting* Duckworth
   Graphology for Everyman Duckworth
   A Handwriting Quiz Book Duckworth
   The Graphologist's Alphabet Duckworth
Stein Lewinson, Thea and Zubin, Joseph *Handwriting Analysis* Kings Crown Press, New
   York
Teillard, Ania *L'Âme et l'Écriture* A. Francke A.G. Verlag, Berne
Teltscher, Dr Herry O. *Handwriting – Revelation of Self* Hawthorne, New York
Victor, Frank *Handwriting – A Personality Projection* Thomas, Illinois
Wolff, Werner *Diagrams of the Unconscious* Grune & Stratton, New York

INDEX

Page references in italics indicate illustrations.